Integrated Math 1

Practice Workbook

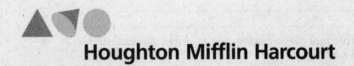

Houghton Mifflin Harcourt

Printed in the U.S.A.

ISBN   978-0-544-71650-6
3 4 5 6 7 8 9 10   0982   25 24 23 22 21 20 19 18
4500705619   B C D E F G

Contents

Student Worksheets

Solving Equations
Practice and Problem Solving: A/B

Use the guess-and-check method to solve. Show your work.

1. $x + 8 = 11$

2. $5y - 9 = 16$

_____ _____

Solve by working backward. Show your work.

3. $x - 4 = 9$

4. $3y + 4 = 10$

_____ _____

Solve the equation by using the Properties of Equality.

5. $6c + 3 = 45$

6. $11 - a = -23$

_____ _____

7. $\dfrac{2}{3} + y = \dfrac{1}{4}$

8. $\dfrac{7}{8}w = 14$

_____ _____

Solve.

9. Houston, Texas has an average annual rainfall about 5.2 times that of El Paso, Texas. If Houston gets about 46 inches of rain, about how many inches does El Paso get? Round to the nearest tenth.

_____

10. Susan can run 2 city blocks per minute. She wants to run 60 blocks. How long will it take her to finish if she has already run 18 blocks?

_____

11. Michaela pays her cell phone service provider $49.95 per month for 500 minutes. Any additional minutes used cost $0.15 each. In June, her phone bill is $61.20. How many additional minutes did she use?

_____

Solving Equations

Practice and Problem Solving: C

Use the guess-and-check method to solve. Show your work.

1. $26 = t - 19$

2. $w - 2 = -43$

_____   _____

Solve by working backward. Show your work.

3. $8n + 6 = 46$

4. $15 - 3y = -3$

_____   _____

Solve the equation by using the Properties of Equality.

5. $2(8 + k) = 22$

6. $m + 5(m - 1) = 7$

_____   _____

7. $-13 = 2b - b - 10$

8. $\dfrac{2}{3}x - \dfrac{5}{8}x = 26$

_____   _____

Solve.

9. Sam is moving into a new apartment. Before he moves in, the landlord asks that he pay the first month's rent and a security deposit equal to 1.5 times the monthly rent. The total that Sam pays the landlord before he moves in is $3275. What is the monthly rent?

_____

10. Mr. Rodriguez invests half his money in land, a tenth in stocks, and a twentieth in bonds. He puts the remaining $35,000 in his savings account. What is the total amount of money that Mr. Rodriguez saves and invests?

_____

11. A work crew has a new pump and an old pump. The new pump can fill a tank in 5 hours, and the old pump can fill the same tank in 7 hours. Write and solve an equation for the time it will take both pumps to fill one tank if the pumps are used together.

_____

LESSON 1-2 Modeling Quantities
Practice and Problem Solving: A/B

Use ratios to solve the problems.

The diagram below represents a tree and a mailbox and their shadows. The heights of the triangles represent the heights of the objects, and the longer sides represent their shadows.

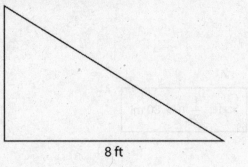
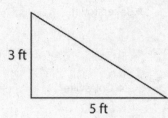

8 ft

3 ft

5 ft

1. What is the height of the tree? _____

Use the diagram below for 2–5.

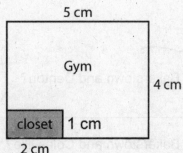

5 cm

Gym

4 cm

closet 1 cm

2 cm

2. If 1 cm represents 10 m, what are the actual measurements of the gym including the closet? _____

3. What are the actual measurements of the closet? _____

4. If 1 cm represents 12 m, what are the actual measurements of the gym including the closet? _____

5. What is the area of the gym? _____

Solve.
Selena rides her bicycle to work. It takes her 15 minutes to go 3 miles.

6. If she continues at the same rate, how long will it take her to go 8 miles?

_____

7. How many feet will she travel in 3 minutes?

_____

Name _____ Date _____ Class_____

LESSON
1-2

Modeling Quantities
Practice and Problem Solving: C

Use a ruler to measure the distance to solve.

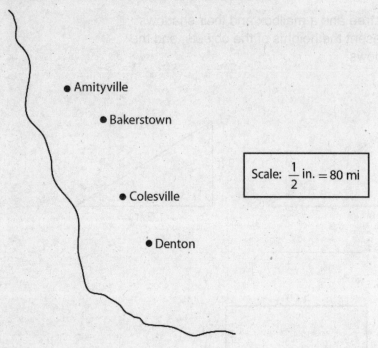

• Amityville

• Bakerstown

Scale: $\frac{1}{2}$ in. = 80 mi

• Colesville

• Denton

1. What is the distance between Bakerstown and Denton?

   _____

2. What is the distance between Bakerstown and Colesville?

   _____

3. If Sarah drives 55 miles per hour, how long will it take her to drive from
   Amityville to Denton?

   _____

4. Hector drives 60 miles an hour from Amityville to Eaglecroft. If it takes
   him 5 hours and 45 minutes, what is the distance between the two cities?

   _____

5. If the scale of the map changes, and the new distance between
   Amityville and Denton is 325 miles, what is the new scale?

   _____

Name _____ Date _____ Class_____

Reporting with Precision and Accuracy

LESSON 1-3

Practice and Problem Solving: A/B

Identify the more precise measurement.

1. 16 ft; 6 in.

2. 4.8 L; 2 mL

3. 4 pt; 1 gal

_____   _____   _____

4. 9.3 mg; 7.05 mg

5. 74 mm; 2.25 cm

6. 12 oz; 11 lb

_____   _____   _____

Find the number of significant digits in each example.

7. 52.9 km

8. 800 ft

9. 70.09 in.

_____   _____   _____

10. 0.6 mi

11. 23.0 g

12. 3120.58 m

_____   _____   _____

Order each list of units from most precise to least precise.

13. yard, inch, foot, mile

14. gram, centigram, kilogram, milligram

_____   _____

Rewrite each number with the number of significant digits indicated in parentheses.

15. 12.32 lb (2)

16. 1.8 m (1)

17. 34 mi (4)

_____   _____   _____

Solve.

18. A rectangular garden has length of 24 m and width of 17.2 m. Use the correct number of significant digits to write the perimeter of the garden.

_____

19. Kelly is making a beaded bracelet with beads that measure 4 mm and 7.5 mm long. If the bracelet is 15 cm long and Kelly uses the same number of each type bead, about how many beads will she use?

_____

20. When two people each measured a window's width, their results were 79 cm and 786 mm. Are these results equally precise? Explain.

_____

Name _____ Date _____ Class_____

LESSON 1-3

Reporting with Precision and Accuracy
Practice and Problem Solving: C

Choose the most precise measurement in each set.

1. 7.0 cm; 700 cm; 7000 cm   2. 30 cm; 30 m; 32 mm   3. 9.5 lb; 0.1 oz; 4 oz

_____   _____   _____

For each measurement, find the number of significant digits.

4. 800 kg   5. 20.0594 km   6. 0.0009 mm

_____   _____   _____

Rewrite each number with the number of significant digits indicated in parentheses.

7. 0.09 mL (2)   8. 5280 ft (1)   9. 9.006 g (3)

_____   _____   _____

Solve.

10. Explain how someone could say the following: "I used to think that 17 and 17.0 were the same. But now I am beginning to wonder."

_____

_____

11. As part of an experiment, a student combined 3.4 g of one chemical with 0.56 g of a second chemical. He then recorded the combined mass as 4 g. Did the student record the combined mass correctly? Explain.

_____

_____

12. Building lumber is labeled according to the dimensions (in inches) of its cross section. So, a "two-by-four" measures 2 inches by 4 inches, but not exactly. In fact, the cross section of a two-by-four has the smallest dimensions possible, while still legitimately being called a two-by-four. Find those dimensions. Then find the percent by which the cross-sectional area of a two-by-four is less than that of a "true" two-by-four.

_____

_____

_____

LESSON
2-1

Modeling with Expressions

Practice and Problem Solving: A/B

Identify the terms and coefficients of each expression.

1. $4a + 3c + 8$

   terms: _____

   coefficients: _____

2. $9b + 6 + 2g$

   terms: _____

   coefficients: _____

3. $8.1f + 15 + 2.7g$

   terms: _____

   coefficients: _____

4. $7p - 3r + 6 - 5s$

   terms: _____

   coefficients: _____

5. $3m - 2 - 5n + p$

   terms: _____

   coefficients: _____

6. $4.6w - 3 + 6.4x - 1.9y$

   terms: _____

   coefficients: _____

Interpret the meaning of the expression.

7. Frank buys p pounds of oranges for $2.29 per pound and the same number of pounds of apples for $1.69 per pound. What does the expression $2.29p + 1.69p$ represent?

   _____

8. Kathy buys p pounds of grapes for $2.19 per pound and one pound of kiwi for $3.09 per pound. What does the expression $2.19p - 3.09$ represent?

   _____

Write an expression to represent each situation.

9. Eliza earns $400 per week plus $15 for each new customer she signs up. Let c represent the number of new customers Eliza signs up. Write an expression that shows how much she earns in a week.

   _____

10. Max's car holds 18 gallons of gasoline. Driving on the highway, the car uses approximately 2 gallons per hour. Let h represent the number of hours Max has been driving on the highway. Write an expression that shows how many gallons of gasoline Max has left after driving h hours.

    _____

11. A man's age today is three years less than four times the age of his oldest daughter. Let a represent the daughter's age. Write an expression to represent the man's age.

    _____

Modeling with Expressions
Practice and Problem Solving: C

Simplify each expression when you can. Then identify the terms and coefficients of each.

1. $5b + 6d - 5c + 19a$

   terms: _____

   coefficients: _____

2. $4w - 5 + 6(2x + 7) - 19$

   terms: _____

   coefficients: _____

3. $12 + 8r - 3(s - 5) + 15t$

   terms: _____

   coefficients: _____

4. $9g - 2(-h + 3j) + 7 - 8k$

   terms: _____

   coefficients: _____

Write a situation that could be represented by the expression.

5. $3a + 6$, where a = age in years

   _____

6. $5(p + 2)$, where p = the number of points scored

   _____

Write an expression for each situation. Then solve the problem.

7. A man's age today is 2 years more than three times the age his son will be 5 years from now. Let a represent the son's age today. Write an expression to represent the man's age today. Then find his age if his son is now 8 years old.

   _____

8. Let n represent an even integer. Write an expression for the sum of that number and the next three even integers after it. Simplify your expression fully.

   _____

9. A Fahrenheit temperature, F, can be converted to its corresponding Celsius temperature by subtracting 32° from that temperature and then multiplying the result by $\frac{5}{9}$. Write an expression that can be used to convert Fahrenheit temperatures to Celsius temperatures. Then find the Celsius temperature corresponding to 95 °F.

   _____

LESSON 2-2

Creating and Solving Equations
Practice and Problem Solving: A/B

Write an equation for each description.

1. 4 times a number is 16.

   _____

2. A number minus 11 is 12.

   _____

3. $\frac{9}{10}$ times a number plus 6 is 51.

   _____

4. 3 times the sum of $\frac{1}{3}$ of a number and 8 is 11.

   _____

Write and solve an equation to answer each problem.

5. Jan's age is 3 years less than twice Tritt's age. The sum of their ages is 30. Find their ages.

   _____

6. Iris charges a fee for her consulting services plus an hourly rate that is $1\frac{1}{5}$ times her fee. On a 7-hour job, Iris charged $470. What is her fee and her hourly rate?

   _____

7. When angles are complementary, the sum of their measures is 90 degrees. Two complementary angles have measures of $2x - 10$ degrees and $3x - 10$ degrees. Find the measures of each angle.

   _____

8. Bill wants to rent a car. Rental Company A charges $35 per day plus $0.10 per mile driven. Rental Company B charges $25 per day plus $0.15 per mile driven. After how many miles driven will the price charged by each company be the same?

   _____

9. Katie, Elizabeth, and Siobhan volunteer at the hospital. In a week, Katie volunteers 3 hours more than Elizabeth does and Siobhan volunteers 1 hour less than Elizabeth. Over 3 weeks, the number of hours Katie volunteers is equal to the sum of Elizabeth's and Siobhan's volunteer hours in 3 weeks. Complete the table to find out how many hours each person volunteers each week.

Volunteer	Volunteer Hours per week	Volunteer Hours over 3 weeks
Katie		
Elizabeth		
Siobhan		

Name _____ Date _____ Class_____

LESSON 2-2

Creating and Solving Equations

Practice and Problem Solving: C

Write an equation for each description.

1. Eight times the difference of a number and 2 is the same as 3 times the sum of the number and 3.

   _____

2. The sum of −7 times a number and 8 times the sum of the number and 1 is the same as the number minus 7.

   _____

3. The quotient of the difference of a number and 24 divided by 8 is the same as the number divided by 6.

   _____

Write an equation for each situation. Then use the equation to solve the problem.

4. Sierra has a total of 61 dimes and quarters in her piggybank. She has 3 more quarters than dimes. The coins have a total value of $10.90. How many dimes and how many quarters does she have? [Hint: Use the decimal values of the c coins to write an equation.]

   _____

5. Penn used the formula for the sum of the angles inside a polygon: Sum of the interior angles = $(n - 2)180$, where n is the number of angles of the polygon. Penn's answer is 1,980 degrees. How many angles does the polygon have?

   _____

6. Fahrenheit temperature, F, can be found from a Celsius temperature, C, using the formula $F = 1.8C + 32$. Write an equation to find the temperature at which the Fahrenheit and Celsius readings are equal. Then find that temperature.

   _____

7. Amanda, Bryan, and Colin are in a book club. Amanda reads twice as many books as Bryan per month and Colin reads 4 fewer than 3 times as many books as Bryan in a month. In 4 months, the number of books Amanda reads is equal to $\frac{5}{8}$ the sum of the number of books Bryan and Colin read in 4 months. How many books does each person read each month?

Name	Books read in 1 month	Books read in 4 months
Amanda		
Bryan		
Colin		

Name _____ Date _____ Class_____

LESSON **Solving for a Variable**
2-3
Practice and Problem Solving: A/B

Solve the equation for the indicated variable.

1. $x = 3y$ for y

2. $m + 5n = p$ for m

3. $12r - 6s = t$ for r

_____ _____ _____

4. $21 = cd + e$ for d

5. $\dfrac{h}{j} = 15$ for j

6. $\dfrac{f-7}{g} = h$ for f

_____ _____ _____

Solve the formula for the indicated variable.

7. Formula for the perimeter of a rectangle:
$P = 2a + 2b$, for b

8. Formula for the circumference of a circle:
$C = 2\pi r$, for r

_____ _____

9. Formula for the sum of angles of a triangle:
$A + B + C = 180°$, for C

10. Formula for the volume of a cylinder:
$V = \pi r^2 h$, for h

_____ _____

Solve.

11. Jill earns $15 per hour babysitting plus a transportation fee of $5 per job. Write a formula for E, Jill's earnings per babysitting job, in terms of h, the number of hours for a job. Then solve your formula for h.

_____

12. A taxi driver charges a fixed rate of r to pick up a passenger. In addition, the taxi driver charges a rate of m for each mile driven. Write a formula to represent T, the total amount this taxi driver will charge for a trip of n miles.

_____

13. Solve your formula from Problem 12 for m. Then find the taxi driver's hourly rate if his pickup rate is $2 and he charges $19.50 for a 7-mile trip.

_____

14. Describe when the formula for simple interest $I = prt$ would be more useful if it were rearranged.

_____

**LESSON
2-3**

Solving for a Variable

Practice and Problem Solving: C

Solve the equation for the indicated variable.

1. $y = \dfrac{3}{8}(x + 4)$ for x

2. $ab - ac = 2$ for a

3. $h - j = 4(h + j) - 7$ for h

_____

_____

_____

4. $n = m^2 - (n + 3)$

5. $\dfrac{d - e}{3d + e} = e$, for d

6. $\dfrac{q}{r} - 6 = q$, for r

_____

_____

_____

Solve the formula for the indicated variable.

7. Formula for centripetal force:

$F = \dfrac{mv^2}{r}$, for m

8. Formula for the volume of a sphere:

$V = \dfrac{4}{3}\pi r^3$, for r

_____

_____

9. Formula for half the volume of a right

circular cylinder: $V = \dfrac{\pi r^2 h}{2}$, for r

10. Formula for focal length:

$\dfrac{1}{V} = \dfrac{1}{U} + \dfrac{1}{F}$, for U

_____

_____

11. Pythagorean Theorem $a^2 + b^2 = c^2$:

for a

12. Formula for the surface area of

a cone: $S = \pi rs + \pi r^2$, for s

_____

_____

Solve.

13. Kinetic energy, K, equals the product of $\dfrac{1}{2}$, the mass of an object, m,

and the square of its velocity, v. Write a formula for kinetic energy.
Then solve your formula for v.

_____

14. In a circle, area and circumference can be found using the formulas

$A = \pi r^2$ and $C = 2\pi r$, respectively. Write a formula for C in terms of
A. (Your answer should not contain π.)

_____

15. Gina paid $131 for a car stereo on sale for 30% off. There was also
7% sales tax on the purchase. Find the original price of the stereo.

_____

Name _____ Date _____ Class_____

LESSON 2-4

Creating and Solving Inequalities
Practice and Problem Solving: A/B

Write an inequality for the situation.

1. Cara has $25 to buy dry pet food and treats for the animal shelter.
   A pound of dog food costs $2 and treats are $1 apiece. If she buys
   9 pounds of food, what is the greatest number of treats she can buy?

   _____

Solve each inequality for the value of the variable.

2. $2x \geq 6$

   _____

3. $\frac{a}{5} < 1$

   _____

4. $5x + 7 \geq 2$

   _____

5. $5(z + 6) \leq 40$

   _____

6. $5x \geq 7x + 4$

   _____

7. $3(b - 5) < -2b$

   _____

Write and solve an inequality for each problem.

8. By selling old CDs, Sarah has a store credit for $153. A new CD costs
   $18. What are the possible numbers of new CDs Sarah can buy?

   _____

   _____

9. Ted needs an average of at least 70 on his three history tests. He has
   already scored 85 and 60 on two tests. What is the minimum grade
   Ted needs on his third test?

   _____

   _____

10. Jay can buy a stereo either online or at a local store. If he buys online,
    he gets a 15% discount, but has to pay a $12 shipping fee. At the local
    store, the stereo is not on sale, but there is no shipping fee. For what
    regular price is it cheaper for Jay to buy the stereo online?

   _____

   _____

LESSON 2-4

Creating and Solving Inequalities

Practice and Problem Solving: C

Write an inequality for the situation.

1. Miguel is buying 10 blankets for the animal shelter. If shipping each blanket costs $1.50 and Miguel has $75 to spend, what is the greatest amount he can spend for each blanket?

   _____

Solve each inequality.

2. $2(x - 3) + 9 \geq x$

   _____

3. $\frac{1}{2}a - 7 < \frac{2}{3}a - 9$

   _____

4. $-10(9 - 2x) - x \leq 2x - 5$

   _____

5. $8\left(1 - \frac{k}{2}\right) > -5k + 17$

   _____

6. $100 - 5(7 - 5y) > 5(7 + 5y) - 100$

   _____

7. $-6(w + 3) - \frac{3w}{2} \leq -11 - 9w$

   _____

Solve.

8. One car rental company charges $30 per day plus $0.25 per mile driven. A second company charges $40 per day plus $0.10 per mile driven. How many miles must you drive for a one-day rental at the second company to be less expensive than the same rental at the first company? Write an inequality to solve.

   _____

9. To solve the inequality $\frac{2x - 1}{x + 8} > 1$, Hal multiplied both sides by $x + 8$ and then got the solution $x > 9$. Is Hal's work correct?

   _____

10. To solve $3 \geq 5 - 2x$, a student typically uses division by -2 and reverses the direction of the inequality. Show how to solve the inequality without using that step. Hint: Use the Addition Property of Equality.

   _____

**LESSON
2-5**

Creating and Solving Compound Inequalities
Practice and Problem Solving: A/B

Solve each compound inequality and graph the solution.

1. $x > 2$ AND $x - 1 \le 10$

   0 2 4 6 8 10 12

   _____

2. $3x + 1 \ge -8$ AND $2x - 3 < 5$

   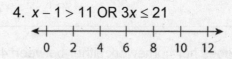

   _____

3. $x > 10$ OR $x < 0$

   0 2 4 6 8 10

   _____

4. $x - 1 > 11$ OR $3x \le 21$

   0 2 4 6 8 10 12

   _____

5. $70 < 3x + 10 < 100$

   0 10 20 30 40

   _____

6. $2 > 2x - 14 > -14$

   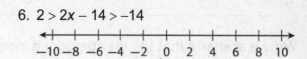

   _____

Write the compound inequality shown by each graph.

7.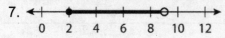

   _____

8.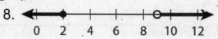

   _____

Write a compound inequality to model the following situations. Graph the solution.

9. The forecast in Juneau, AK, calls for between 1.2 and 2.0 inches of rain.

   1.0 1.5 2.0 2.5 3.0

   _____

10. Water from industrial plants must be treated before entering the sewer system. Water that is too acidic or too basic will harm the pipes. A semiconductor manufacturer must adjust the pH of any waste water from the process to between 4.0 and 10.0.

    0 2 4 6 8 10

    _____

11. A welding shop figures a new welding machine will be cost effective if it runs less than 2 hours or more than 5.5 hours per day.

    0 1 2 3 4 5 6 7 8 9 10

    _____

LESSON
2-5

Creating and Solving Compound Inequalities
Practice and Problem Solving: C

Write the compound inequality, or inequalities. Draw and label a number line and graph the inequalities.

1. Pilots in the U.S. Air Force must meet certain height requirements. They must be at least 5 feet 4 inches tall, but not taller than 6 feet 2 inches. Convert the heights to inches before completing the problem.

_____

2. Julie does her homework either between 4:00 and 6:00 p.m. or between 8:00 and 10:00 p.m.

_____

Write a scenario that fits the compound inequality shown.

3.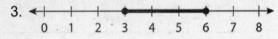

_____

_____

_____

4.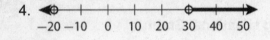

_____

_____

_____

Name _____ Date _____ Class _____

Graphing Relationships

Practice and Problem Solving: A/B

Solve.

1. The graph shows the amount of rainfall during one storm. What does segment *d* represent?

   _____

   _____

2. Which segment represents the heaviest rainfall?

   _____

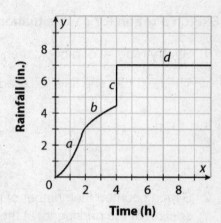

For each situation, tell whether a graph of the situation would be a continuous graph or a discrete graph.

3. the number of cans collected for recycling _____

4. pouring a glass of milk _____

5. the distance a car travels from a garage _____

6. the number of people in a restaurant _____

Identify which graph represents the situation, the kind of graph, and the domain and range of the graph.

7. Jason takes a shower, but the drain in the shower is not working properly.

a.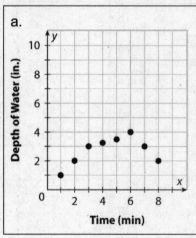

b.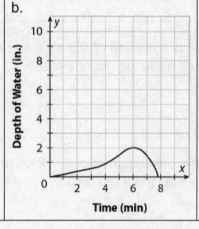

c.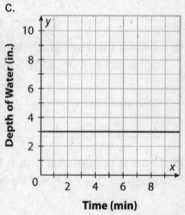

_____

LESSON
3-1

Graphing Relationships

Practice and Problem Solving: C

Sketch a graph for each situation. Be sure to label your graph.

1. Sherry read $\frac{1}{3}$ of a book, then went to bed.

   The next day she finished reading the entire book.

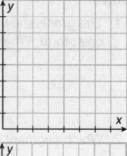

2. Simon counted the number of red trucks in each section of the parking lot at the mall.

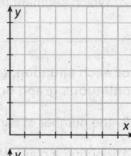

3. On Monday, the furniture truck made three deliveries within 8 miles of the warehouse.

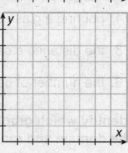

4. Write a situation for which you would use a discrete graph.

   _____

   _____

5. Draw a discrete graph that has a domain of $0 \le x \le 8$ and a range of {2, 4, 6, 8, 10}. Write a situation for the graph.

   _____

   _____

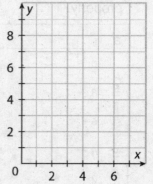

6. Draw a continuous graph that has a domain of $0 \le x \le 5$ and a range of $0 \le x \le 8$. Write a situation for the graph.

   _____

   _____

LESSON 3-2

Understanding Relations and Functions

Practice and Problem Solving: A/B

Express each relation as a table, as a graph, and as a mapping diagram.

1. {(−2, 5), (−1, 1), (3, 1), (−1, −2)}

x	y

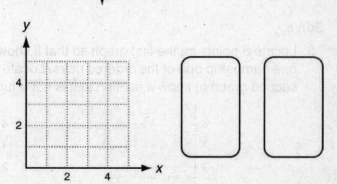

2. {(5, 3), (4, 3), (3, 3), (2, 3), (1, 3)}

x	y

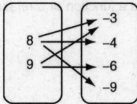

Give the domain and range of each relation. Tell whether the relation is a function. Explain.

3.

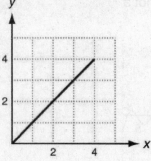

D: _____

R: _____

Function? _____

Explain: _____

_____

_____

4.

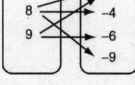

8 → −3, −4
9 → −6, −9

D: _____

R: _____

Function? _____

Explain: _____

_____

_____

5.

x	y
1	4
2	5
0	6
1	7
2	8

D: _____

R: _____

Function? _____

Explain: _____

_____

_____

LESSON 3-2

Understanding Relations and Functions

Practice and Problem Solving: C

Graph each relation. Then explain whether it is a function or not.

1. {(1, 2), (2, 2), (3, 3), (4, 3)}

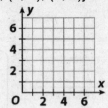

_____

_____

2. {(1, 5), (2, 4), (3, 5), (3, 4), (4, 4), (5, 5)}

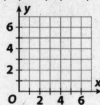

_____

_____

Solve.

3. Locate 5 points on the first graph so that it shows a function. Then change one number in one of the ordered pairs. Locate the new set of points on the second graph to show a relation that is not a function. Explain your strategy.

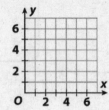   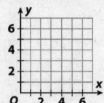

_____

4. Identify whether the graph shows a function or a relation that is not a function. Explain your reasoning.

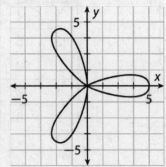   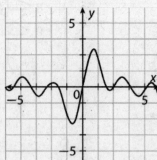

_____

5. The function INT(x) is used in spreadsheet programs. INT(x) takes any x and rounds it down to the nearest integer. Find INT(x) for x = 4.6, −2.3, and $\sqrt{2}$. Then find the domain and range.

_____

LESSON 3-3

Modeling with Functions

Practice and Problem Solving: A/B

Identify the dependent and independent variables in each situation.

1. The cost of a dozen eggs depends on the size of the eggs.

   dependent: _____   independent: _____

2. Ally works in a shop for $18 per hour.

   dependent: _____   independent: _____

3. 5 pounds of apples costs $7.45.

   dependent: _____   independent: _____

For each situation, write a function as a standard equation and in function notation.

4. Keesha will mow grass for $8 per hour.

   standard: _____   function: _____

5. Oranges are on sale for $1.59 per pound.

   standard: _____   function: _____

For each situation, identify the dependent and independent variables. Write a function in function notation, and use the function to solve the problem.

6. A plumber charges $70 per hour plus $40 for the call. What does he charge for 4 hours of work?

   dependent: _____   Solution: _____

   independent: _____   _____

   function: _____   _____

7. A sanitation company charges $4 per bag for garbage pickup plus a $10 weekly fee. A restaurant has 14 bags of *g* garbage. What will the sanitation company charge the restaurant?

   dependent: _____   Solution: _____

   independent: _____   _____

   function: _____   _____

LESSON 3-3

Modeling with Functions
Practice and Problem Solving: C

A range for each function is given. Find the domain values from the list: 1, 2, 3, 4, 5, 6, 7, 8. Explain how you arrived at your answer.

1. Function: $f(x) = -4x - 8$ R: {−16, −28, −36, −40}

   D: _____

   Explain: _____

   _____

2. Function: $f(x) = \frac{3}{2}x - 17$ R: {−15.5, −12.5, −9.5, −8}

   D: _____

   Explain: _____

   _____

3. Function: $f(x) = -\frac{1}{4}x + 2$ R: {1.5, 1, 0.25, 0}

   D: _____

   Explain: _____

   _____

4. Function: $f(x) = -5x - 13$ R: {−28, −38, −43, −48}

   D: _____

   Explain: _____

   _____

Solve.

5. A bakery has prepared 320 ounces of bread dough. A machine will cut the dough into 5-ounce sections and bake each section into a loaf. The amount of d dough left after m minutes is given by the function $d(m) = -5m + 320$. How many minutes will it take the machine to use all the dough? Find a reasonable domain and range for this situation.

   _____

   _____

LESSON 3-4

Graphing Functions

Practice and Problem Solving: A/B

Complete the table and graph the function for the given domain.

1. $f(x) = 3x - 2$ for D = {-3, 1, 5}

x	y
-3	
1	
5	

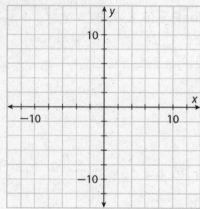

2. $y + 2x = 12$ for D = {2, 3, 4}

x	y
2	
3	
4	

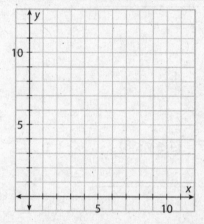

3. $3x - 3y = 9$ for D = {0 ≤ x ≤ 8}

x	y
0	
3	
8	

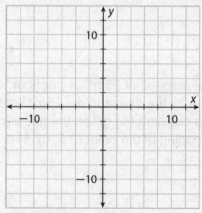

4. The function $h(d) = 2d + 4.3$ relates the h height of the water in a fountain in feet to the d diameter of the pipe carrying the water. Graph the function on a calculator and use the graph to find the height of the water when the pipe has a diameter of 1.5 inches.

_____

LESSON 3-4

Graphing Functions

Practice and Problem Solving: C

Determine the domain for each function. Then graph the function.

1. $f(x) = \frac{1}{2}x + 4$ for R = {5, 6, 7, 8}

   D = _____

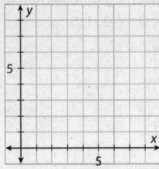

2. $6x - 3y = 12$ for R = {−4 ≤ y ≤ 8}

   D = _____

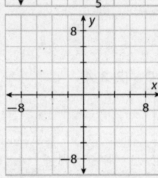

3. $3x = y - 4$ for R = {4 ≤ y ≤ 8}

   D = _____

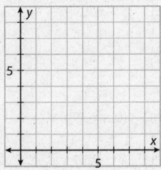

Solve.

4. A car travels at a speed of 25 miles per hour. The *d* distance it travels in *h* hours is given by the equation $d = 25h$. Write the equation as a function. Use a calculator to graph the function for the domain {0 ≤ h ≤ 5}. What is the meaning of the point (3.5, 87.5) on the graph?

   Function: _____

   Explain: _____

5. The formula for finding the distance traveled by a free-falling object is $D = 16t^2$, where *t* is the time in seconds. Use a calculator to graph this function for the domain {1, 2, 3, 4, 5, 6}. Find the range. Use the graph to find how much time it takes the object to fall 300 feet.

   Range: _____

   Explain: _____

LESSON 4-1 Identifying and Graphing Sequences

Practice and Problem Solving: A/B

Complete the table and state the domain and range for the sequence.

1.

n	1	2	☐	4	☐	6
f(n)	12	☐	36	☐	60	☐

Domain: _____

Range: _____

Write the first four terms of each sequence.

2. $f(n) = 3n - 1$

3. $f(n) = n^2 + 2n + 5$

_____   _____

4. $f(n) = (n-1)(n-2)$

5. $f(n) = \sqrt{n-1}$

Emma pays $10 to join a gym. For the first 5 months she pays a monthly $15 membership fee. For problems 6–7, use the explicit rule $f(n) = 15n + 10$.

6. Complete the table.

7. Graph the sequence using the ordered pairs.

n	$f(n) = 15n + 10$	f(n)
1	$f(1) = 15\,(1) + 10 = 25$	25
2	$f(\Box) = 15\,(\Box) + \Box = \Box$	☐
3	$f(\Box) = 15\,(\Box) + \Box = \Box$	☐
4	$f(\Box) = 15\,(\Box) + \Box = \Box$	☐
5	$f(\Box) = 15\,(\Box) + \Box = \Box$	☐

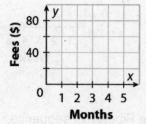

Use the table to create ordered pairs.
The ordered pairs are

_____

_____

Name _____ Date _____ Class_____

LESSON 4-1

Identifying and Graphing Sequences

Practice and Problem Solving: C

Find the first four terms of each sequence.

1. $f(n) = n^3 - n^2 + 1$

   _____

2. $f(n) = \dfrac{1}{n} - \dfrac{1}{n+1}$

   _____

3. $f(n) = \dfrac{n(n+1)(2n+1)}{6}$

   _____

4. $f(n) = \dfrac{n^2 - 1}{n^2 + 1}$

   _____

5. $f(n) = \dfrac{n}{12} - \dfrac{2}{3}$

   _____

6. $f(1) = 9$, $f(n) = 13 + \sqrt{f(n-1)}$ for $n \geq 2$

   _____

Graph the sequence that represents the situation on a coordinate plane.

7. Rebecca had $100 in her savings account in the first week. She adds $45 each week for 5 weeks. The savings account balance can be shown by a sequence.

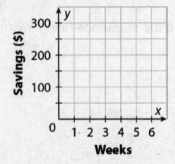

8. Adam has $300 to donate. For the next five weeks he donates $60 each week to a different charity. His remaining donation money can be shown by a sequence.

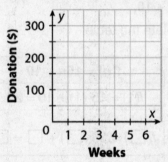

Solve.

9. In the Fibonacci sequence, $f(1) = 1$, $f(2) = 1$, and $f(n) = f(n-2) + f(n-1)$ for $n \geq 3$. Find the first 10 terms of the Fibonacci sequence.

   _____

10. Use $f(n)$ from Problem 9 to create a new sequence: $r(n) = \dfrac{f(n)}{f(n+1)}$.

    Write the first eight terms of this sequence as decimals. If necessary, round a term to three decimal places. Explain any patterns you see.

    _____

LESSON 4-2 Constructing Arithmetic Sequences

Practice and Problem Solving: A/B

Write an explicit rule and a recursive rule using the table.

1.

n	1	2	3	4	5
f(n)	8	12	16	20	24

_____

_____

2.

n	1	2	3	4	5
f(n)	11	7	3	−1	−5

_____

_____

3.

n	1	2	3	4	5
f(n)	−20	−13	−6	1	8

_____

_____

4.

n	1	2	3	4	5
f(n)	2.7	4.3	5.9	7.5	9.1

_____

_____

Write an explicit rule and a recursive rule using the sequence.

5. 45, 50, 55, 60, 65

_____

_____

6. 94, 87, 80, 73, 66

_____

_____

7. 12, 26, 40, 54, 68

_____

_____

8. 83, 43, 3, −37, −77

_____

_____

Solve.

9. The explicit rule for an arithmetic sequence is $f(n) = 13 + 6(n - 1)$.
   Find the first four terms of the sequence.

_____

10. Helene paid back $100 in Month 1 of her loan. In each month after that,
    Helene paid back $50. The graph shows the sequence. Write an explicit rule.

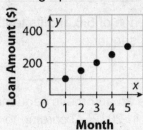

_____

Constructing Arithmetic Sequences
Practice and Problem Solving: C

Write an explicit rule and a recursive rule for each sequence.

1.

n	1	2	3	4	5
$f(n)$	−3.4	−2.1	−0.8	0.5	1.8

2.

n	1	2	3	4	5
$f(n)$	$\frac{1}{6}$	$\frac{1}{4}$	$\frac{1}{3}$	$\frac{5}{12}$	$\frac{1}{2}$

3.

n	1	3	5	6	9
$f(n)$	82	81	80	79.5	78

4.

n	1	4	8	13	19
$f(n)$	−22	2	34	74	122

Solve.

5. A recursive rule for an arithmetic sequence is $f(1) = -8$, $f(n) = f(n-1) - 6.5$ for $n \geq 2$. Write an explicit rule for this sequence.

6. The third and thirtieth terms of an arithmetic sequence are 4 and 85. Write an explicit rule for this sequence.

7. $f(n) = 900 - 60(n-1)$ represents the amount Oscar still needs to repay on a loan at the beginning of month n. Find the amount Oscar pays monthly and the month in which he will make his last payment.

8. Find the first six terms of the sequence whose explicit formula is $f(n) = (-1)^n$. Explain whether it is an arithmetic sequence.

9. An arithmetic sequence has common difference of 5.6 and its tenth term is 75. Write a recursive formula for this sequence.

10. The cost of a college's annual tuition follows an arithmetic sequence. The cost was $35,000 in 2010 and $40,000 in 2012. According to this sequence, what will tuition be in 2020?

LESSON 4-3
Modeling with Arithmetic Sequences
Practice and Problem Solving: A/B

Complete the table of values to determine the common difference.

1. Mia drives 55 miles per hour. The total miles driven is given by the function $C(m) = 55m$.

Hours	1	2	3	4
Distance in miles				

Common difference: _____

2. Each pound of potatoes costs $1.20. The total cost, in dollars, is given by the function $C(p) = 1.2p$.

Pounds	1	2	3	4
Cost in dollars				

Common difference: _____

Solve. Use the following for 3–7.

Riley buys a swim pass for the pool in January. The first month costs $30. Each month after that, the cost is $20 per month. Riley wants to swim through December.

3. Complete the table of values.

Months	1	2	3	4	5	6	7	8	9	10	11	12
Cost in dollars	30	50	70									

4. What is the common difference?

_____

5. Write the equation for finding the total cost of a one-year swim pass.

_____

6. What does $f(12)$ represent?

_____

7. What is the total amount of money Riley will spend for a one-year swim pass?

_____

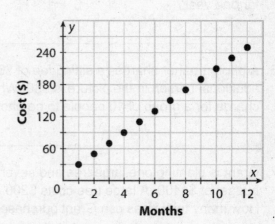

Modeling with Arithmetic Sequences
Practice and Problem Solving: C

Use the following diagram for 1–3.

       _____

   1   **2**   **3**   **4**   **5**   **6**   **7**   **8**

1. How many sides will Figure 8 have? Is it shaded?

   _____

2. Make a table to show the sequence of figures.

Figure					
Number of Sides					

3. How many sides will Figure 21 have? Is it shaded?

   _____

4. Is the sequence of figures an arithmetic sequence? Explain.

   _____

Solve.

5. A movie rental club charges $4.95 for the first month's rentals. The club charges $18.95 for each additional month. What is the total cost for one year?

   _____

6. A photographer charges a sitting fee of $69.95 for one person. Each additional person in the picture is $30. What is the total sitting fee charge for a group of 10 people to be photographed?

   _____

7. Grant is planting one large tree and several smaller trees. He has a budget of $1400. A large tree costs $200. Each smaller tree is $150. How many total trees can Grant purchase on his budget?

   _____

LESSON 5-1

Understanding Linear Functions

Practice and Problem Solving: A/B

Tell whether each function is linear or not.

1. $y = 3x^2$

2. $7 - y = 5x + 11$

3. $-2(x + y) + 9 = 1$

_____   _____   _____

Complete the tables. Is the change constant for equal intervals?
If so, what is the change?

4. $3x + 5y = 4$

x	−1	0	1	2
y	$\frac{7}{5}$			

Constant? _____

Change? _____

5. $4x^2 + y = 4$

x	−1	0	1	2
y	0	4		

Constant? _____

Change? _____

6. $6x + 1 = y$

x	−1	0	1	2
y				

Constant? _____

Change? _____

Graph each line.

7. $y = \frac{1}{2}x - 3$

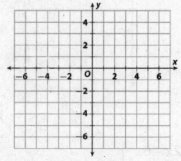

8. $2x + 3y = 8$

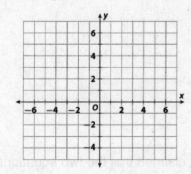

The solid and dashed lines show how two
consultants charge for their services. Use the graph
for 9–11.

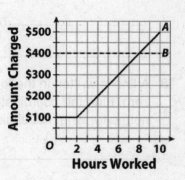

9. How much does each charge for a 6-hour job?

_____

10. Does either consultant charge according to a linear function?

_____

11. For which length of job do *A* and *B* charge the same amount?

_____

12. Are the functions discrete or continuous? Explain. _____

LESSON 5-1

Understanding Linear Functions

Practice and Problem Solving: C

Tell what constant amount the function changes by over equal intervals.

1. $3x + 4y = 24$

2. $y = -5x + 10$

_____

3. $x - 7y - 15 = 0$

4. $9x - \dfrac{2}{3}y = -4$

_____

Graph each line.

5. $6x + 5y = 30$

6. $3(x + y) - 2(x - y) = 5(8 + 3y)$

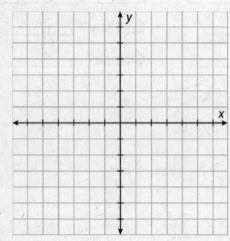

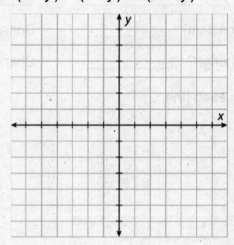

Solve.

7. A student claimed that the two equations $\dfrac{y-8}{x-1} = 2$ and $y = 2x + 6$ have identical lines as their graphs. Do you agree? Explain.

_____

_____

8. A line is written in the form $Ax + By = 0$, where A and B are not both zero. Find the coordinates of the point that must lie on this line, no matter what the choice of A and B.

_____

_____

9. A line is written in the form $Ax + By = C$, where $A \neq 0$. Find the x-coordinate of the point on the line at which $y = 3$.

_____

_____

LESSON
5-2

Using Intercepts

Practice and Problem Solving: A/B

Find each *x*- and *y*-intercept.

1.
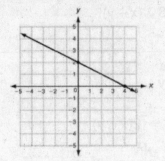

_____

_____

2.
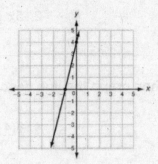

_____

_____

3.
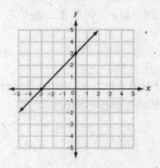

_____

_____

Use intercepts to graph the line described by each equation.

4. $3x + 2y = -6$

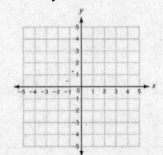

5. $x - 4y = 4$

6. At a fair, hamburgers sell for $3.00 each and hot dogs sell for
$1.50 each. The equation $3x + 1.5y = 30$ describes the number
of hamburgers and hot dogs a family can buy with $30.

  a. Find the intercepts and graph the function.

    _____

  b. What does each intercept represent?

    _____

    _____

    _____

    _____

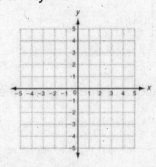

LESSON
5-2

Using Intercepts
Practice and Problem Solving: C

Find each *x*- and *y*-intercept.

1. $4(x - y) + 3 = 2x - 5$

2. $5x + 9y = 18 - (x + y)$

_____

_____

Find each *x*- and *y*-intercept. Then graph the line described by each equation.

3. $x - (y + 2) = 3(x - 2y + 1)$

4. $8(4 + x) - 3 = 12(x + y) + 5$

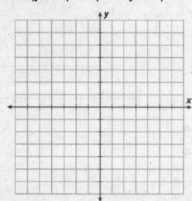

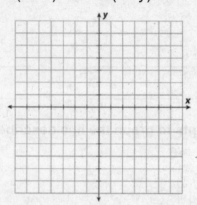

Solve.

5. Write the equations of three distinct lines that have the same *y*-intercept, –1.

_____

6. A home uses 8 gallons of oil each day for heat. If its oil storage tank is filled to 275 gallons, the function $y = 275 - 8x$ represents the number of gallons remaining in the tank after *x* days of use. Explain what the *x*-intercept represents. Then determine when the tank will be half-full.

_____

_____

7. The *x*-intercept of a line is twice as great as its *y*-intercept. The sum of the two intercepts is 15. Write the equation of the line in standard form.

_____

8. A linear equation has more than one *y*-intercept. What can you conclude about the graph of the equation?

_____

LESSON 5-3

Interpreting Rate of Change and Slope

Practice and Problem Solving: A/B

Find the rise and run between the marked points on each graph. Then find the rate of change or slope of the line.

1.
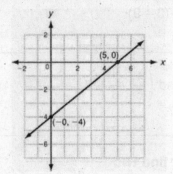

2.
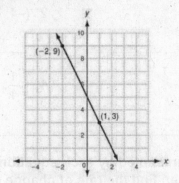

3.
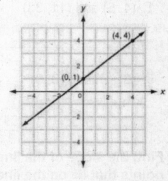

rise = _____ run = _____   rise = _____ run = _____   rise = _____ run = _____

slope = _____   slope = _____   slope = _____

Find the slope of each line. Tell what the slope represents.

4.
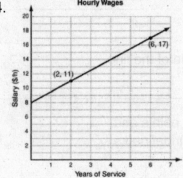

5.
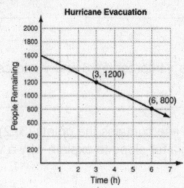

_____   _____

_____   _____

Solve.

6. When ordering tickets online, a college theater charges a $5 handling fee no matter how large the order. Tickets to a comedy concert cost $58 each. If you had to graph the line showing the total cost, *y*, of buying *x* tickets, what would the slope of your line be? Explain your thinking.

_____

_____

_____

LESSON 5-3

Interpreting Rate of Change and Slope
Practice and Problem Solving: C

Find the rate of change or slope of the line containing each pair of points.

1. (4, 5) and (11, 33)

2. (−4, 8) and (3, −9)

_____

_____

3. (0, −8) and (3, 3)

4. $\left(\dfrac{1}{4}, \dfrac{1}{2}\right)$ and $\left(\dfrac{1}{6}, \dfrac{1}{3}\right)$

_____

_____

Find the slope of the line represented by each equation. First find two points that lie on the line. Then find the rate of change or slope.

5. $2x + y = 5$

6. $3x − 5y = 17$

7. $y = 4 − 9x$

_____

_____

_____

8. $y + 5 = 1$

9. $−x + 4y = 12$

10. $6(x − y) = 5(x + y)$

_____

_____

_____

Solve.

11. A line has *x*-intercept of 6 and *y*-intercept of −4. Find the slope of the line.

_____

12. A vertical line contains the points (3, 2) and (3, 6). Use these points and the formula for slope to explain why a vertical line's slope is undefined.

_____

_____

13. The steepness of a road is called its grade. The higher the grade, the steeper the road. For example, an interstate highway is considered out of standard if its grade exceeds 7%. Interpret a grade of 7% in terms of slope. Use feet to explain the meaning for a driver.

_____

_____

14. Ariel was told the *x*-intercept and the *y*-intercept of a line with a positive slope. Yet, it was impossible for Ariel to find the slope of the line. What can you conclude about this line? Explain your thinking.

_____

_____

LESSON 6-1
Slope-Intercept Form
Practice and Problem Solving: A/B

Write the equation for each line in slope-intercept form. Then identify the slope and the *y*-intercept.

1. $4x + y = 7$

   Equation: _____

   Slope: _____

   y-intercept: _____

2. $2x - 3y = 9$

   Equation: _____

   Slope: _____

   y-intercept: _____

3. $5x + 1 = 4y + 7$

   Equation: _____

   Slope: _____

   y-intercept: _____

4. $3x + 2y = 2x + 8$

   Equation: _____

   Slope: _____

   y-intercept: _____

Graph the line described by each equation.

5. $y = -3x + 4$

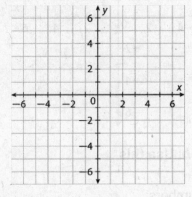

6. $y = \frac{5}{6}x - 1$

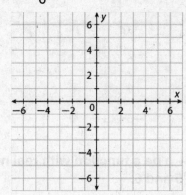

Solve.

7. What are the slope and *y*-intercept of $y = 3x - 5$?

   _____

8. A line has a *y*-intercept of −11 and slope of 0.25. Write its equation in slope-intercept form.

   _____

9. A tank can hold 30,000 gallons of water. If 500 gallons of water are used each day, write the equation that represents the amount of water in the tank *x* days after it is full.

   _____

LESSON 6-1

Slope-Intercept Form

Practice and Problem Solving: C

Write the equation for each line in slope-intercept form. Then identify the slope and the *y*-intercept.

1. $3(x - 2y) = 5(x - 3y) + 9$

   Equation: _____

   Slope: _____

   y-intercept: _____

2. $\dfrac{x}{5} - \dfrac{y}{7} = 1$

   Equation: _____

   Slope: _____

   y-intercept: _____

Write an equation for each line. Then graph the line.

3. A line whose slope and *y*-intercept are equal and the sum of the two is –4

   _____

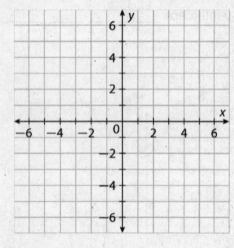

4. A line that has a slope half as great as its *y*-intercept and the sum of the two is 1

   _____

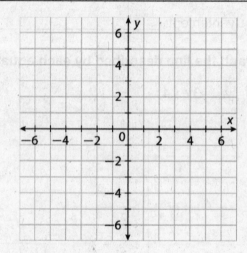

Let $f(x) = mx + b$ be a function with real numbers for *m* and *b*. Use this for Problems 5 and 6.

5. Show that the domain of this function is the set of all real numbers.

   _____

   _____

6. Show that the range of the function may or may not be the set of all real numbers.

   _____

   _____

   _____

   _____

LESSON 6-2

Point-Slope Form

Practice and Problem Solving: A/B

Write each in point-slope form.

1. Line with a slope of 2 and passes through point (3, 5).

   _____

2. Line with a slope of −3 and passes through point (−1, 7).

   _____

3. (−6, 3) and (4, 3) are on the line.

   _____

4. (0, 0) and (5, 2) are on the line.

   _____

5.

x	y
0	0
2	9
4	18

6.

x	y
−2	18
1	9
4	0

7.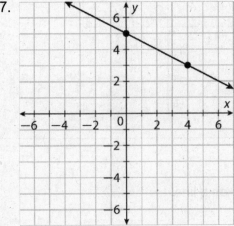

   _____

8.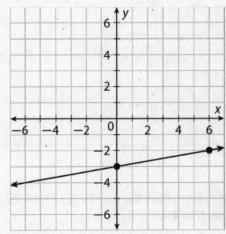

   _____

Solve.

9. For 4 hours of work, a consultant charges $400. For 5 hours of work, she charges $450. Write a point-slope equation to show this, then find the amount she will charge for 10 hours of work.

   _____

   _____

LESSON 6-2

Point-Slope Form

Practice and Problem Solving: C

Write each in point-slope form.

1. The graph of the function has slope of $-\dfrac{3}{4}$ and contains $\left(-2, -\dfrac{8}{5}\right)$.

   _____

2. The graph of the function has slope of $\dfrac{2}{5}$ and contains $(-35, 39)$.

   _____

3.

x	y
$\dfrac{1}{6}$	−5
$\dfrac{1}{2}$	−10

_____

4.

x	y
1	$-\dfrac{2}{3}$
$\dfrac{2}{3}$	2

_____

5.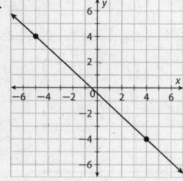

_____

6.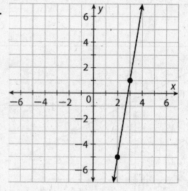

_____

Solve.

7. Ben claims that the points (2, 4), (4, 8), and (8, 12) lie on a line. Show that Ben is incorrect.

   _____

   _____

8. Prove the following statement: If the *x*- and *y*-intercepts of a line are identical nonzero numbers, the line must have a slope of −1.

   _____

   _____

9. A consignment store charges a flat rate plus a percent of the sale price for any items it sells. An item priced at $500 carries a total fee of $120 while an item priced at $800 carries a total fee of $180. Use the point-slope equation to find the total fee for an item priced at $300.

   _____

LESSON
6-3

Standard Form
Practice and Problem Solving: A/B

Tell whether each function is written in standard form. If not, rewrite it in standard form.

1. $y = 3x$

2. $7 - y = 5x + 11$

3. $-2(x + y) + 9 = 1$

_____   _____   _____

_____   _____   _____

Given a slope and a point, write an equation in standard form for each line.

4. slope = 6, (3, 7)

5. slope = −1, (2, 5)

6. slope = 9, (−5, 2)

_____   _____   _____

Graph the line of each equation.

7. $x - 2y = 6$

8. $2x + 3y = 8$

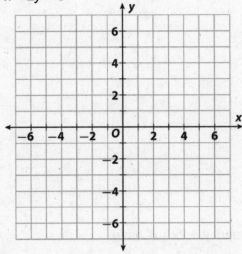

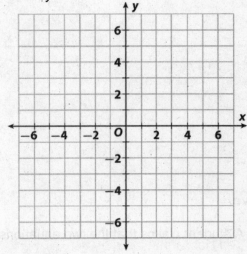

Solve.

9. A swimming pool was filling with water at a constant rate of 200 gallons per hour. The pool had 50 gallons before the timer started. Write an equation in standard form to model the situation.

_____

10. A grocery bag containing 4 potatoes weighs 2 pounds. An identical bag that contains 12 potatoes weighs 4 pounds. Write an equation in standard form that shows the relationship of the weight (*y*) and the number of potatoes (*x*).

_____

LESSON 6-3 Standard Form

Practice and Problem Solving: C

Write each equation in slope-intercept form. Then identify its intercepts.

1. $3x + 4y = 24$

2. $y = -5x + 10$

_____

_____

3. $x - 7y - 15 = 0$

4. $9x - \dfrac{2}{3}y = -4$

_____

_____

Graph each line. Rewrite the equation in standard form if necessary.

5. $6x + 5y = 30$

6. $3(x + y) - 2(x - y) = 5(8 + 3y)$

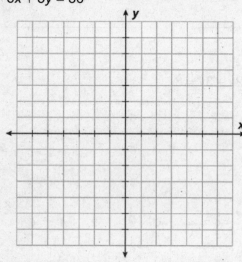
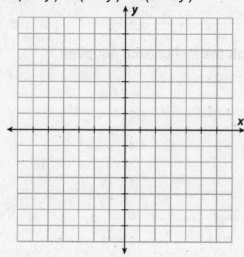

Solve.

7. A student claims that the two equations $\dfrac{y - 8}{x - 1} = 2$ and $y = 2x + 6$ have

   identical lines as their graphs. Do you agree? Explain.

_____

_____

8. A line is written in standard form $Ax + By = 0$, where A and B are not
   both zero. Find the coordinates of the point that must lie on this line, no
   matter what the choice of A and B.

_____

9. A line is written in standard form $Ax + By = C$, where $A \neq 0$. Find the
   x-coordinate of the point on the line at which $y = 3$.

_____

LESSON
6-4

Transforming Linear Functions

Practice and Problem Solving: A/B

Identify the steeper line.

1. $y = 3x + 4$ or $y = 6x + 11$

_____

2. $y = -5x - 1$ or $y = -2x - 7$

_____

Each transformation is performed on the line with the equation
$y = 2x - 1$. Write the equation of the new line.

3. vertical translation down 3 units

_____

4. slope increased by 4

_____

5. slope divided in half

_____

6. shifted up 1 unit

_____

7. slope increased by 50%

_____

8. shifted up 3 units and slope doubled

_____

A salesperson earns a base salary of $4000 per month plus 15%
commission on sales. Her monthly income, $f(s)$, is given by the
function $f(s) = 4000 + 0.15s$, where s is monthly sales, in dollars.
Use this information for Problems 9–12.

9. Find $g(s)$ if the salesperson's commission is lowered to 5%.

_____

10. Find $h(s)$ if the salesperson's base salary is doubled.

_____

11. Find $k(s)$ if the salesperson's base salary is cut in half and her
commission is doubled.

_____

12. Graph $f(s)$ and $k(s)$ on the coordinate grid below.

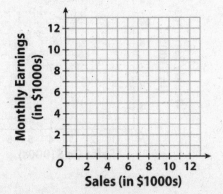

LESSON 6-4
Transforming Linear Functions
Practice and Problem Solving: C

Identify the steeper line.

1. $y = 2x - 3$ or $x - 5y = 20$

_____

2. $x + 10y = 1$ or $3x + 20y = 1$

_____

Each transformation is performed on the line with the equation
$y = 4x - 20$. **Write the equation of the new line.**

3. slope cut in half

_____

4. vertical translation 25 units upward

_____

5. shifted up 8 units and slope tripled

_____

6. reflection across the y-axis

_____

Solve.

7. Compare the steepness of the lines whose equations are $8x + y = 1$ and $-8x + y = 2$. Explain your reasoning.

_____

_____

8. $f(x)$ is an increasing linear function that passes through the point (4, 0). Show that if written in the form $f(x) = mx + b$, $m > 0$ and $b < 0$.

_____

_____

9. A salesperson earns a base salary of $400 per week plus 20% commission on sales. He is offered double his base salary if he'll accept half his original commission. Graph and label the original deal and the new deal below. Next to the graph, find when the original deal is a better choice. Explain your thinking.

_____

_____

_____

_____

Name _____ Date _____ Class_____

Comparing Properties of Linear Functions
Practice and Problem Solving: A/B

The linear functions *f(x)* and *g(x)* are defined by the graph and table below. Assume that the domain of *g(x)* includes all real numbers between the least and greatest values of *x* shown in the table.

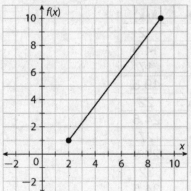

x	g(x)
1	35
2	30
3	25
4	20
5	15
6	10
7	5
8	0

1. Find the domain of *f(x)*.

_____

2. Find the domain of *g(x)*.

_____

3. Find the range of *f(x)*.

_____

4. Find the range of *g(x)*.

_____

5. Find the initial value of *f(x)*.

_____

6. Find the initial value of *g(x)*.

_____

7. Find the slope of the line represented by *f(x)*.

_____

8. Find the slope of the line represented by *g(x)*.

_____

9. How are *f(x)* and *g(x)* alike? How are they different?

_____

10. Describe a situation that could be represented by *f(x)*.

_____

11. Describe a situation that could be represented by *g(x)*.

_____

12. If the domains of *f(x)* and *g(x)* were extended to include all real numbers greater than or equal to 0, what would their *y*-intercepts be?

_____

LESSON 6-5

Comparing Properties of Linear Functions
Practice and Problem Solving: C

The linear functions *f*(*x*), *g*(*x*), *h*(*x*), and *k*(*x*) are defined by the graphs and table below. Assume that the domains of *h*(*x*) and *k*(*x*) include all real numbers between the least and greatest values of *x* shown in the table.

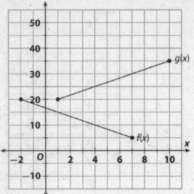

x	h(x)	k(x)
1	2.5	12
2	5	14.5
3	7.5	17
4	10	19.5
5	12.5	22
6	15	24.5
7	17.5	27
8	20	29.5
9	22.5	32
10	25	34.5

1. Find the domains of the functions.

   _____

2. Find the ranges of the functions.

   _____

3. Find the initial values of the functions.

   _____

4. Find the slopes of the functions.

   _____

5. Describe a situation that could be represented by two of the functions.

   _____

6. If the domains of the functions were extended to include all real
   numbers greater than or equal to 0, what would their *y*-intercepts be?

   _____

7. If the domain of *f*(*x*) and *g*(*x*) were extended to include all real
   numbers, at what point would their graphs intersect?

   _____

LESSON
7-1
Modeling Linear Relationships
Practice and Problem Solving: A/B

Solve.

1. A recycling center pays $0.10 per aluminum can and $0.05 per plastic bottle. The cheerleading squad wants to raise $500.

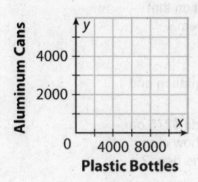

   a. Write a linear equation that describes the problem.

   _____

   b. Graph the linear equation.

   c. If the cheerleading squad collects 6000 plastic bottles, how many cans will it need to collect to reach the goal?

   _____

2. A bowling alley charges $2.00 per game and will rent a pair of shoes for $1.00 for any number of games. The bowling alley has an earnings goal of $300 for the day.

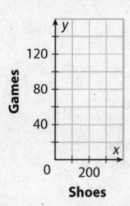

   a. Write a linear equation that describes the problem.

   _____

   b. Graph the linear equation.

   c. If the bowling alley rents 40 pairs of shoes, how many games will need to be played to reach its goal?

   _____

3. The members of a wheelchair basketball league are playing a benefit game to meet their fundraising goal of $900. Tickets cost $15 and snacks cost $6.

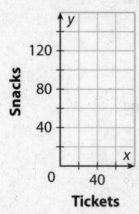

   a. Write a linear equation that describes the problem.

   _____

   b. Graph the linear equation.

   c. If the team sells 50 tickets, how many snacks does it need to sell to reach the goal?

   _____

LESSON 7-1

Modeling Linear Relationships

Practice and Problem Solving: C

Solve.

1. Mr. Malone can heat his house in the winter by burning three cords of wood, by using natural gas, or by a combination of the two. His heating budget for the winter is $600.

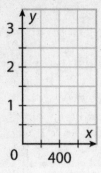

a. Write a linear equation that describes the problem.

_____

b. Graph the linear equation and label both axes.

c. If Mr. Malone spends $275 on natural gas, about how many cords of wood will he need?

_____

2. Timber Hill Tennis Club sells monthly memberships for $72 and tennis rackets for $150 each. The tennis club has a sales goal of $5400 per month.

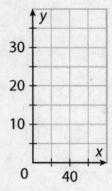

a. Write a linear equation that describes the problem.

_____

b. Graph the linear equation and label both axes.

c. If the club sells 50 memberships, how many rackets must be sold to meet the goal?

_____

3. Brian's Bakery sells loaves of Italian bread for $3.50 and loaves of rye bread for $2.80. Brian's goal is to bring in $420 per day from sales of these two items.

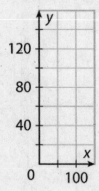

a. Write a linear equation that describes the problem.

_____

b. Graph the linear equation and label both axes.

c. If Brian sells 100 Italian loaves, how many rye loaves must he sell to meet his goal?

_____

LESSON 7-2

Using Functions to Solve One-Variable Equations

Practice and Problem Solving: A/B

Use the following for 1–5.

Locksmith Larry charges $90 for a house call plus $20 per hour.
Locksmith Barry charges $50 for a house call plus $30 per hour.

1. Write a one-variable equation for the charges of Locksmith Larry.

   $f(x) = $ _____

2. Write a one-variable equation for the charges of Locksmith Barry.

   $g(x) = $ _____

3. Complete the table for $f(x)$ and $g(x)$.

Hours	$f(x)$	$g(x)$
0		
1		
2		
3		
4		
5		

4. Plot $f(x)$ and $g(x)$ on the graph below. Find the intersection.

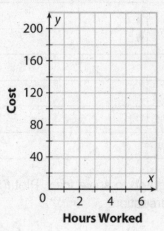

5. After how many hours will the two locksmiths charge the same

   amount? _____

6. Jill has $600 in savings. She has a recurring monthly bill of $75 but no income.

   a. Write an equation, $f(x)$, representing her savings each month.

   _____

   b. Let $g(x) = 0$ represent the point when Jill has no money left. In how many months, x, will her savings account reach zero?

   _____

Using Functions to Solve One-Variable Equations

LESSON 7-2

Practice and Problem Solving: C

Use the following for 1–5.

DJ A charges $75.30 plus $12.50 per hour. DJ B charges $52.90 plus $18.10 per hour. When will their charges be equal?

1. Write a one-variable equation for the charges of DJ A.

   $f(x) =$ _____

2. Write a one-variable equation for the charges of DJ B.

   $g(x) =$ _____

3. Complete the table for $f(x)$ and $g(x)$.

Hours	$f(x)$	$g(x)$
0		
1		
2		
3		
4		
5		

4. Use a graph to solve for *x*. Plot $f(x)$ and $g(x)$ on the graph below. Find the intersection.

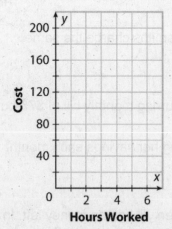

5. After how many hours will the two DJs charge the same

   amount? _____

LESSON 7-3

Linear Inequalities in Two Variables

Practice and Problem Solving: A/B

Use substitution to tell whether each ordered pair is a solution of the given inequality.

1. $(3, 4); y > x + 2$

2. $(4, 2); y \leq 2x - 3$

3. $(2, -1); y < -x$

_____   _____   _____

Rewrite each linear inequality in slope-intercept form. Then graph the solutions in the coordinate plane.

4. $y - x \leq 3$

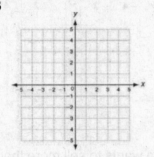

5. $6x + 2y > -2$

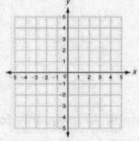

_____   _____

6. Trey is buying peach and blueberry yogurt cups. He will buy at most 8 cups of yogurt. Let x be the number of peach yogurt cups and y be the number of blueberry yogurt cups he buys.

   a. Write an inequality to describe the situation.

   _____

   b. Graph the solutions.

   c. Give two possible combinations of peach and blueberry yogurt that Trey can choose.

   _____

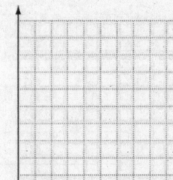

Write an inequality to represent each graph.

7.

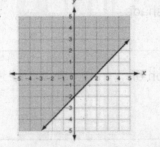

8.

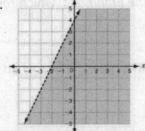

9.

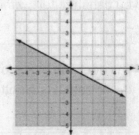

_____   _____   _____

LESSON
7-3

Linear Inequalities in Two Variables
Practice and Problem Solving: C

Graph the solution set for each inequality.

1. $2x - 3y \le 15$

2. $\dfrac{1}{4}x + \dfrac{1}{3}y < \dfrac{1}{2}$

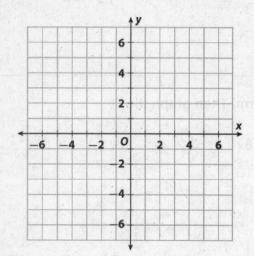 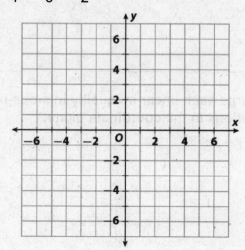

Write and graph an inequality for each situation.

3. Hats (x) cost $5 and scarves ($y$) cost $8. Joel can spend at most $40.

4. Juana wants to sell more than 1 million dollars worth of $1000 laptops ($x$) and $2000 desktop computers ($y$) this year.

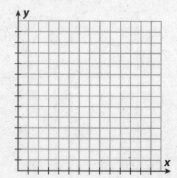 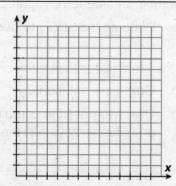

Solve.

5. To graph $y \le 2x + 8$, you first draw the line $y = 2x + 8$. Explain how you can then tell, *without doing any arithmetic,* which region to shade.

_____

6. Why does the graph of $y \ge x$ contain a solid line while the graph of $y > x$ contains a dotted line?

_____

Two-Way Frequency Tables

Practice and Problem Solving: A/B

Solve.

1. Nancy's school conducted a recycling drive. Students collected 20-pound bags of plastic, glass, and metal containers. The first chart shows the data: the bags of each type of container that were collected. Complete the frequency table.

20-pound Bags Collected
glass glass plastic metal
plastic plastic metal glass
glass plastic metal metal
metal glass glass plastic
plastic plastic plastic metal

Bags containing	Frequency
plastic	
glass	

2. A school administrator conducted a survey in her school. Students were asked to choose the science or the natural history museum for an upcoming field trip. Complete the two-way frequency table.

	Field Trip Preferences		
Gender	**Science**	**History**	**Total**
Boys		56	102
Girls	54		
Total			200

3. Teresa surveyed 100 students about whether they wanted to join the math club or the science club. Thirty-eight students wanted to join the math club only, 34 wanted to join the science club only, 21 wanted to join both math and science clubs, and 7 did not want to join either. Complete the two-way frequency table.

	Science		
Math	**Yes**	**No**	**Total**
Yes		38	
No	34		
Total			

4. A pet-shop owner surveyed 200 customers about whether they own a cat or a dog. Partial results of the survey are recorded below. Complete the two-way frequency table.

   One-half of the respondents own a dog but not a cat.

   The number of customers who own neither a dog nor a cat is 38.

   There are no customers who own both a dog and a cat.

	Cat		
Dog	**Yes**	**No**	**Total**
Yes	0		
No		38	
Total			

Name ______________________ Date ____________ Class ____________

LESSON 8-1

Two-Way Frequency Tables

Practice and Problem Solving: C

1. A surveyor asked students whether they favored or did not favor a change in the Friday lunch menu at their school.
   - The survey involved 200 students.
   - The number of boys surveyed equaled the number of girls surveyed.
   - Fifty percent of the girls favored the change.
   - The number of boys who did not favor the change was two-thirds of the number of boys who favored the change.

   Complete the two-way frequency table. Explain your reasoning.

	Favor or Disfavor the Change		
Gender	**Yes**	**No**	**Total**
Girls			
Boys			
Total			

____

____

____

2. A pet-shop owner surveyed 150 customers about whether they owned birds, cats, or dogs. Partial results of the survey are recorded below. In the table, B represents bird, C represents cat, and D represents dog.

	Ownership								
Reply	**B**	**C**	**D**	**B and C Only**	**B and D Only**	**C and D Only**	**B, C, D**	**Not B, C, or D**	**Total**
Yes	80	77	84	32	30	29	12	6	150
No	70	73	66	128	120	121	138	144	150
Total	150	150	150	150	150	150	150	150	150

Write the correct number in each of the eight regions in the Venn diagram below.

Pet Owners in the Survey

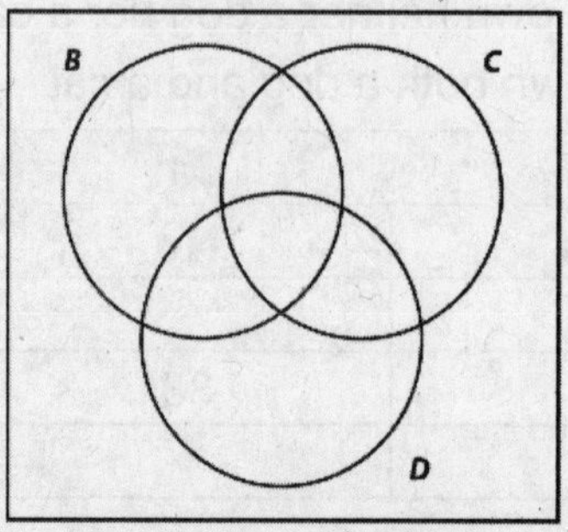

Relative Frequency

Practice and Problem Solving: A/B

The two-way frequency table below represents the results of a survey about favorite forms of entertainment. In Exercises 1–3, write fractions that are not simplified as responses.

	Like Board Games		
Like Reading	**Yes**	**No**	**Total**
Yes	48	25	73
No	43	9	52
Total	91	34	125

1. Find the joint relative frequency of people surveyed who like to read but dislike playing board games. _____

2. What is the marginal relative frequency of people surveyed who like to read? _____

3. Given someone interested in reading, is that person more or less likely to take an interest in playing board games? Explain.

   _____

   _____

4. Given someone interested in board games, is that person more or less likely to take an interest in reading? Explain your response.

   _____

   _____

The two-way frequency table below represents the results of a survey about ways students get to school.

	Type of Transportation			
Grade	**On Foot**	**By Car**	**By Bus**	**Total**
9	15	28	64	107
10	20	30	43	93
Total	35	58	107	200

5. Find the joint relative frequency of students surveyed who walk to school and are in grade 9. _____

6. Given grade level, is that person more or less likely to travel to school by bus? Explain your response.

   _____

   _____

   _____

Name _____ Date _____ Class_____

Relative Frequency

Practice and Problem Solving: C

LESSON 8-2

The two-way frequency table below represents the results of a survey about men, women, and televised sports.

1. Complete the table.

	Like Televised Sports		
Gender	**Yes**	**No**	**Total**
Men	48		73
Women	43	9	
Total		34	125

In Exercise 2–5, write your answers as percents.

2. Find the joint relative frequency of men surveyed who like televised sports. _____

3. Find the marginal relative frequency of people surveyed who like televised sports. _____

4. Given someone is male, is that person more or less likely to like televised sports? Explain.

   _____

   _____

5. Given someone likes televised sports, is that person more or less likely to be male? Explain your response.

   _____

   _____

The two-way frequency table below represents the results of a survey about ways people get to the movies.

6. Complete the table.

	Type of Transportation			
Age	**On Foot**	**By Car**	**By Bus**	**Total**
Adult	15	28	64	
Child		30	43	93
Total	35		107	

7. Find the joint relative frequency of people surveyed who walk to the movies and are adults. _____

8. Given that a person is an adult, is that person more or less likely to travel to the movies by bus? What about if the person is a child? Explain your response.

   _____

   _____

   _____

LESSON 9-1 Measures of Center and Spread

Practice and Problem Solving: A/B

Find the mean, median, and range for each data set.

1. 18, 24, 26, 30

    Mean: _____

    Median: _____

    Range: _____

2. 5, 5, 9, 11, 13

    Mean: _____

    Median: _____

    Range: _____

3. 72, 91, 93, 89, 77, 82

    Mean: _____

    Median: _____

    Range: _____

4. 1.2, 0.4, 1.2, 2.4, 1.7, 1.6, 0.9, 1.0

    Mean: _____

    Median: _____

    Range: _____

The data sets below show the ages of the members of two clubs. Use the data for 5–9.

Club A: 42, 38, 40, 34, 35, 48, 38, 45
Club B: 22, 44, 43, 63, 22, 27, 58, 65

5. Find the mean, median, range, and interquartile range for Club A.

    _____

6. Find the mean, median, range, and interquartile range for Club B.

    _____

7. Find the standard deviation for each club. Round to the nearest tenth.

    _____

8. Use your statistics to compare the ages and the spread of ages on the two clubs.

    _____

    _____

9. Members of Club A claim that they have the "younger" club. Members of Club B make the same claim. Explain how that could happen.

    _____

    _____

Name _____ Date _____ Class_____

Measures of Center and Spread
Practice and Problem Solving: C

The data sets below show the price that a homeowner paid, per therm, for natural gas during each of the first ten months of 2011 and 2012. Use the data for 1–4.

2011: $1.59, $1.72, $1.71, $1.86, $2.32, $2.54, $2.45, $2.80, $2.38, $2.25
2012: $1.57, $1.61, $1.96, $1.71, $1.98, $2.17, $2.51, $2.44, $2.52, $2.10

1. Find the mean, median, range, and interquartile range for 2011.

   _____

2. Find the mean, median, range, and interquartile range for 2012.

   _____

3. Find the standard deviation for each year. Round to the nearest hundredth.

   _____

4. Use your statistics to compare the overall trend in prices for the two years.

   _____

   _____

   _____

Solve.

5. To earn an exemption from the final exam, Aaron needs his mean test score to be 92 or greater. If Aaron scored 90, 96, 87, and 90 on the first four tests and he has one test still to take, what is the lowest he can score and still earn an exemption?

   _____

6. *A*, *B*, and *C* are positive integers with $A < B < C$. The mean of *A*, *B*, and *C* is 25, and their median is 10. Find all possible values for *C*.

   _____

7. A teacher gave a test to 24 students and recorded the scores as a data set. Afterward, the teacher realized that the total number of points on the test added up to 96 instead of 100. To correct this, she added four points to each student's score. How did the mean, median, range, interquartile range, and standard deviation change from the original data set of scores when she added four points to each score?

   _____

LESSON
9-2

Data Distributions and Outliers
Practice and Problem Solving: A/B

For each data set, determine if 100 is an outlier. Explain why or why not.

1. 60, 68, 100, 70, 78, 80, 82, 88

2. 70, 75, 77, 78, 100, 80, 82, 88

_____

_____

_____

_____

The table below shows a major league baseball player's season home run totals for the first 14 years of his career. Use the data for Problems 3–8.

Season	1	2	3	4	5	6	7	8	9	10	11	12	13	14
Home Runs	18	22	21	28	30	29	32	40	33	34	28	29	22	20

3. Find the mean and median.

4. Find the range and interquartile range.

_____

_____

5. Make a dot plot for the data.

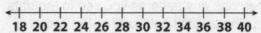

18 20 22 24 26 28 30 32 34 36 38 40

6. Examine the dot plot. Do you think any of the season home run totals are outliers? Then test for any possible outliers.

_____

_____

7. The player wants to predict how many home runs he will hit in his 15th season. Could he use the table or the dot plot to help him predict? Explain your reasoning.

_____

_____

_____

8. Suppose the player hits 10 home runs in his 15th season. Which of the statistics from Problems 3 and 4 would change?

_____

Data Distributions and Outliers

LESSON 9-2

Practice and Problem Solving: C

For each data set, determine if 100 is an outlier. Explain why or why not.

1. 90, 56, 78, 82, 75, 68, 88, 100, 75   2. 123, 111, 122, 100, 109, 117, 125, 121, 130

_____   _____

_____   _____

The table below shows the age of 20 presidents of the United States upon first taking office. Use the data for Problems 3–8.

54	42	51	56	55	51	54	51	60	62
43	55	56	61	52	69	64	46	54	47

3. Find the mean and median.   4. Find the range and interquartile range.

_____   _____

5. Make a dot plot for the data.

6. Examine the dot plot. Describe any patterns you see in the data. Could these patterns be seen in the original data set?

_____

_____

_____

7. Examine the dot plot. Test for any possible outliers.

_____

_____

_____

8. The most recent president of the United States not included in the data set above was Grover Cleveland, who took office on March 4, 1893. Based on your work so far, make an educated guess as to his age that day. Explain your reasoning. Then find his age.

_____

Name _____ Date _____ Class_____

LESSON 9-3

Histograms and Box Plots

Practice and Problem Solving: A/B

Solve each problem.

1. The number of calls per day to a fire and rescue service for three weeks is given below. Use the data to complete the frequency table.

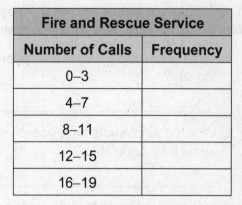

Fire and Rescue Service	
Number of Calls	Frequency
0–3	
4–7	
8–11	
12–15	
16–19	

Calls for Service										
5	17	2	12	0	6	3	8	15	1	4
19	16	8	2	11	13	18	3	10	6	

2. Use the frequency table in Exercise 1 to make a histogram with a title and axis labels.

3. Which intervals have the same frequency?

   _____

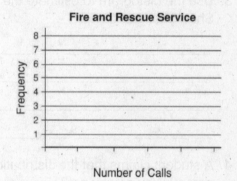

4. Use the histogram to estimate the mean. Then compare your answer with the actual mean, found by using the original data.

   _____

   _____

Use the box plot for Problems 5–7.

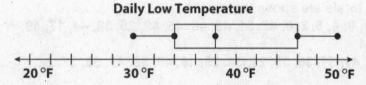

Daily Low Temperature

5. Find the median temperature.

   _____

6. Find the range.

   _____

7. Determine whether the temperature of 50 °F is an outlier.

   _____

   _____

Histograms and Box Plots

Practice and Problem Solving: C

LESSON 9-3

The histogram below shows the population distribution, by age, for the city of Somerville. Use the histogram to solve the problems that follow.

1. What is the approximate total population of the city?

   _____

2. Which age intervals have approximately the same total population?

   _____

3. Use the histogram to estimate the mean age. Show your work.

   _____

   _____

   _____

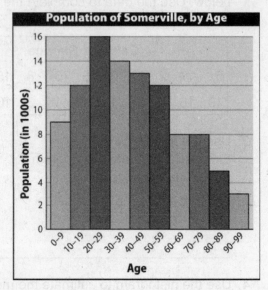

4. A student claims that the distribution is roughly symmetric. Do you agree? Why or why not?

   _____

   _____

Use the data for Problems 5–7. Harmon Killebrew and Willie Mays were two of baseball's all-time greatest home run hitters. Their season home run totals are shown below.
Harmon Killebrew: 0, 4, 5, 2, 0, 42, 31, 46, 48, 45, 49, 25, 39, 44, 17, 49, 41, 28, 26, 5, 13, 14
Willie Mays: 20, 4, 41, 51, 36, 35, 29, 34, 29, 40, 49, 38, 47, 52, 37, 22, 23, 13, 28, 18, 8, 6

5. Make a double box plot for Killebrew and Mays.

   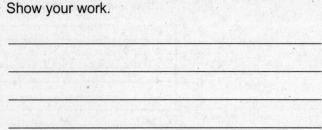

6. Find mean and median season home run totals for Killebrew and Mays.

   _____

LESSON 9-4

Normal Distributions
Practice and Problem Solving: A/B

A collection of data follows a normal distribution. Find the percent of the data that falls within the indicated range of the mean.

1. one standard deviation of the mean

_____

2. three standard deviations of the mean

_____

3. two standard deviations above the mean

_____

4. one standard deviation below the mean

_____

The amount of cereal in a carton is listed as 18 ounces. The cartons are filled by a machine, and the amount filled follows a normal distribution with mean of 18 ounces and standard deviation of 0.2 ounce. Use this information for 5–7.

5. Find the probability that a carton of cereal contains less than its listed amount.

_____

6. Find the probability that a carton of cereal contains between 18 ounces and 18.4 ounces.

_____

7. Find the probability that a carton of cereal contains between 17.6 ounces and 18.2 ounces.

_____

Suppose the manufacturer of the cereal above is concerned about your answer to Problem 5. A decision is made to leave the amount listed on the carton as 18 ounces while increasing the mean amount filled by the machine to 18.4 ounces. The standard deviation remains the same. Use this information for 8–11.

8. Find the probability that a carton contains less than its listed amount.

_____

9. Find the probability that a carton contains more than its listed amount.

_____

10. Find the probability that a carton now contains more than 18.2 ounces.

_____

11. Find the probability that a carton is more than 0.2 ounce under the weight listed on the carton.

_____

Name _____ Date _____ Class _____

Normal Distributions
Practice and Problem Solving: C

When a fair coin is tossed, it has a probability *p* of 0.5 that it will land showing Heads. If the coin is tossed *n* times, it can land showing Heads anywhere from 0 to *n* times.

1. Find the probability that a fair coin tossed *n* times will never land showing Heads. Evaluate for *n* = 5 and write as a percent.

   _____

2. Suppose a fair coin is tossed 1000 times. If you had to predict the number of times it will land showing Heads, what would your prediction be? Justify your answer.

   _____

The number of Heads obtained when a coin is tossed *n* times obeys a probability rule called the Binomial Distribution. For large *n*, this rule can be approximated using a normal distribution. In the case of a fair coin, the mean is 0.5*n* and the standard deviation is $0.5\sqrt{n}$. Use the normal distribution to estimate the following probabilities.

3. The probability that a fair coin tossed 100 times lands showing Heads between 45 and 55 times

   _____

4. The probability that a fair coin tossed 100 times lands showing Heads fewer than 45 times

   _____

5. The probability that a fair coin tossed 100 times lands showing Heads more than 65 times

   _____

6. The probability that a fair coin tossed 2500 times lands showing Heads between 1200 and 1300 times

   _____

Solve.

7. A coin is tossed 400 times as part of an experiment and lands showing Heads 221 times. A student concludes that this is not a fair coin. What do you think? Justify your reasoning.

   _____

   _____

   _____

Name _____ Date _____ Class_____

Scatter Plots and Trend Lines
Practice and Problem Solving: A/B

Graph a scatter plot and find the correlation.

1. The table shows the number of juice drinks sold at a small restaurant from 11:00 am to 1:00 pm. Graph a scatter plot using the given data.

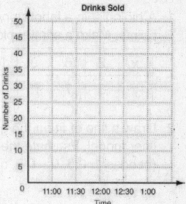
Drinks Sold

Time	11:00	11:30	12:00	12:30	1:00
Number of Drinks	20	29	34	49	44

2. Name the two variables. _____

3. Write *positive*, *negative*, or *none* to describe the correlation illustrated by the scatter plot you drew in problem 1. Estimate the value of the correlation coefficient, *r*. Indicate whether *r* is closer to –1, –0.5, 0, 0.5, or 1.

_____

A city collected data on the amount of ice cream sold in the city each day and the amount of suntan lotion sold at a nearby beach each day.

4. Do you think there is causation between the city's two variables? If so, how? If not, is there a third variable involved? Explain.

_____

Solve.

5. The number of snowboarders and skiers at a resort per day and the amount of new snow the resort reported that morning are shown in the table.

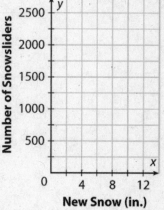

Amount of New Snow (in inches)	2	4	6	8	10
Number of Snowsliders	1146	1556	1976	2395	2490

   a. Make a scatterplot of the data.

   b. Draw a line of fit on the graph above and find the equation
   for the linear model. _____

   c. If the resort reports 15 inches of new snow, how many skiers and snowboarders would you expect to be at the resort that day?

_____

Name _____ Date _____ Class_____

LESSON
10-1

Scatter Plots and Trend Lines

Practice and Problem Solving: C

Graph a scatter plot and find the correlation.

1. A biologist in a laboratory comes up with the following data
points. Make a scatter plot using the data in the table.

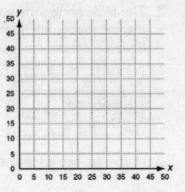

x	2	6	9	14	16	21	25	28
y	3	7	15	33	38	35	40	41

2. Draw a line of fit on the graph and find the equation for the
liner model. Estimate the correlation coefficient, *r*
(choose 1, 0.5, 0, –0.5, or –1).

_____   _____

3. Use a graphing calculator to find the equation for the line of best fit for
the data presented in the table above. Use a graphing calculator to find
the correlation coefficient, *r*.

_____   _____

4. Compare the results you found in step 3, using a graphing calculator,
to those you found in step 2, estimating. The calculator provides a line
of BEST fit, while the line you drew by hand is called a line of fit.
Explain the difference.

_____

_____

_____

LESSON 10-2
Fitting a Linear Model to Data
Practice and Problem Solving: A/B

The table below lists the ages and heights of 10 children. Use the data for 1–5.

A, age in years	2	3	3	4	4	4	5	5	5	6
H, height in inches	30	33	34	37	35	38	40	42	43	42

1. Draw a scatter plot and line of fit for the data.

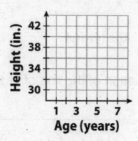

2. A student fit the line $H = 3.5A + 23$ to the data. Graph the student's line above. Then calculate the student's predicted values and residuals.

A, age in years	2	3	3	4	4	4	5	5	5	6
H, height in inches	30	33	34	37	35	38	40	42	43	42
Predicted Values										
Residuals										

3. Use the graph below to make a residual plot.

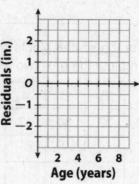

4. Use your residual plot to discuss how well the student's line fits the data.

_____

_____

5. Use the student's line to predict the height of a 20-year-old man. Discuss the reasonableness of the result.

_____

_____

Name _____ Date _____ Class_____

Fitting a Linear Model to Data
Practice and Problem Solving: C

Use the scatter plot, fitted line, and residual plot for 1–5.

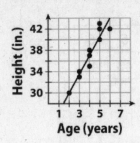 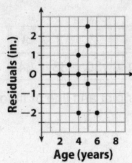

1. Find the equation of the line of fit shown above.

   _____

2. Use the line of fit to predict the height of a 20-year old man. Discuss
   the suitability of the linear model for extrapolation in this case.

   _____

   _____

3. Examine the residual plot. Does the distribution seem suitable?
   Discuss any issues you see.

   _____

   _____

4. The data for the scatter plot is shown in the first two rows of the table
   below. Complete the next two rows of the table.

A	2	3	3	4	4	4	5	5	5	6
H	30	33	34	37	35	38	40	42	43	42
AH										
A^2										

5. The row sums in the table above can be used to find a line of fit. This
   line is called the least-squares line of best fit. Use these formulas to
   find the slope and *y*-intercept of that line:

   $$m = \frac{10 \cdot \text{sum}(AH) - \text{sum}(A) \cdot \text{sum}(H)}{10 \cdot \text{sum}(A^2) - (\text{sum}(A))^2}$$

   _____

   _____

   $$b = \frac{\text{sum}(H) \cdot \text{sum}(A^2) - \text{sum}(A) \cdot \text{sum}(AH)}{10 \cdot \text{sum}(A^2) - (\text{sum}(A))^2}$$

   _____

Name _____ Date _____ Class_____

Solving Linear Systems by Graphing
Practice and Problem Solving: A/B

Tell the number of solutions for each system of two linear equations and state if the system is consistent or inconsistent and dependent or independent.

1.

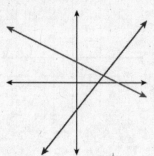

_____

_____

_____

2.

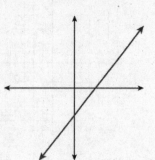

_____

_____

_____

3.

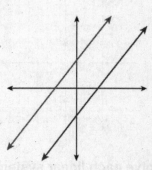

_____

_____

_____

Solve each system of linear equations by graphing.

4. $\begin{cases} x + y = 3 \\ -x + y = 1 \end{cases}$

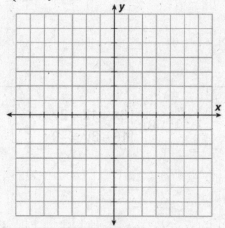

solution: _____

5. $\begin{cases} 6x + 3y = 12 \\ 8x + 4y = 24 \end{cases}$

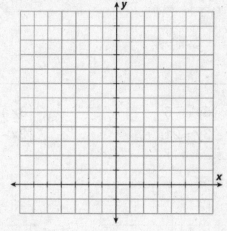

solution: _____

6. Jill babysits and earns *y* dollars at a rate of $8 per hour plus a $5 transportation fee. Samantha babysits and earns *2y* dollars at $16 per hour plus a $10 transportation fee. Write a system of equations and graph to determine the number of hours each needs to babysit to earn the same amount of money.

_____

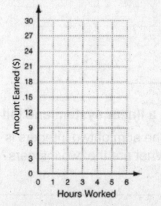

LESSON
11-1

Solving Linear Systems by Graphing

Practice and Problem Solving: C

Draw a graph of a system of linear equations that is:

1. consistent and independent
2. consistent and dependent
3. inconsistent

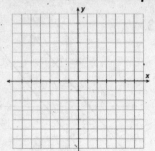 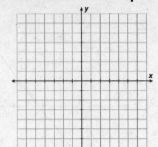 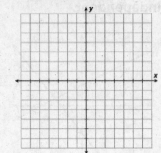

Solve each linear system by graphing. State if there is no solution or an infinite number of solutions.

4. $\begin{cases} 4x + 3y = 9 \\ 2x + y = 4 \end{cases}$

5. $\begin{cases} 4x - 5y = 20 \\ 8x - 12 = 10y \end{cases}$

6. $\begin{cases} x + 3y = 6 \\ 3x + 9y = 18 \end{cases}$

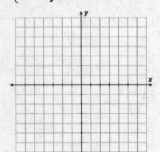 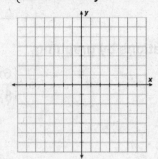 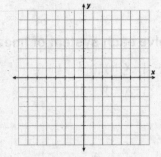

_____ _____ _____

7. $\begin{cases} x - 3y = -6 \\ x - 3y = 21 \end{cases}$

8. $\begin{cases} 3x + y = 4 \\ 2x - 2y = 8 \end{cases}$

9. $\begin{cases} 6x + 12 = 2y \\ 18 - 3y = -9x \end{cases}$

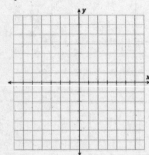 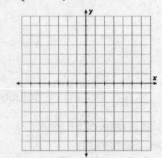 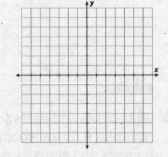

_____ _____ _____

Write a linear system and tell how to solve by graphing.

10. The sum of two integers is 12 and the difference of the two integers is 6. What are the two integers?

_____

LESSON 11-2
Solving Linear Systems by Substitution
Practice and Problem Solving: A/B

Solve each system by substitution. Check your answer.

1. $\begin{cases} y = x - 2 \\ y = 4x + 1 \end{cases}$

2. $\begin{cases} y = x - 4 \\ y = -x + 2 \end{cases}$

3. $\begin{cases} y = 3x + 1 \\ y = 5x - 3 \end{cases}$

_____   _____   _____

4. $\begin{cases} 2x - y = 6 \\ x + y = -3 \end{cases}$

5. $\begin{cases} 2x + y = 8 \\ y = x - 7 \end{cases}$

6. $\begin{cases} 2x + 3y = 0 \\ x + 2y = -1 \end{cases}$

_____   _____   _____

7. $\begin{cases} 3x - 2y = 7 \\ x + 3y = -5 \end{cases}$

8. $\begin{cases} -2x + y = 0 \\ 5x + 3y = -11 \end{cases}$

9. $\begin{cases} \dfrac{1}{2}x + \dfrac{1}{3}y = 5 \\ \dfrac{1}{4}x + y = 10 \end{cases}$

_____   _____   _____

Write a system of equations to solve.

10. A woman's age is three years more than twice her son's age. The sum of their ages is 84. How old is the son?

_____

11. The length of a rectangle is three times its width. The perimeter of the rectangle is 100 inches. What are the dimensions of the rectangle?

_____

12. Benecio worked 40 hours at his two jobs last week. He earned $20 per hour at his weekday job and $18 per hour at his weekend job. He earned $770 in all. How many hours did he work at each job?

_____

13. Choose one of Exercises 1–9 and graph its solution.

Does the answer you found by substitution agree with the answer you got by graphing?

_____

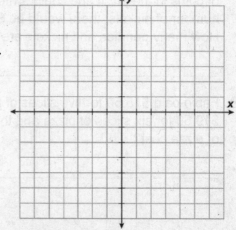

LESSON 11-2

Solving Linear Systems by Substitution

Practice and Problem Solving: C

Solve each system by substitution. Check your answer.

1. $\begin{cases} 4x - 9y = 1 \\ 2x + y = -5 \end{cases}$

2. $\begin{cases} \dfrac{1}{2}x + y = 2 \\ \dfrac{2}{3}x - \dfrac{1}{4}y = 28 \end{cases}$

3. $\begin{cases} 2x + 4y = 1 \\ x + 6y = 1 \end{cases}$

_____   _____   _____

Write a system of equations to solve.

4. Aaron is three times as old as his son. In ten years, Aaron will be twice as old as his son. How old is Aaron now?

_____

5. Kitara has 100 quarters and dimes. Their total value is $19. How many of each coin does Kitara have?

_____

6. A cleaning company charges a fixed amount for a house call and a second amount for each room it cleans. The total cost to clean six rooms is $250 and the total cost to clean eight rooms is $320. How much would this company charge to clean two rooms?

_____

7. Willie Mays and Mickey Mantle hit 88 home runs one season to lead their leagues. Mays hit 14 more home runs than Mantle that year. How many home runs did Willie Mays hit?

_____

8. Coco has a jar containing pennies and nickels. There is $9.20 worth of coins in the jar. If she could switch the number of pennies with the number of nickels, there would be $26.80 worth of coins in the jar. How many pennies and nickels are in the jar?

_____

9. Fabio paid $15.50 for five slices of pizza and two sodas. Liam paid $19.50 for six slices of pizza and three sodas. How much does a slice of pizza cost?

_____

LESSON 11-3

Solving Linear Systems by Adding or Subtracting
Practice and Problem Solving: A/B

Solve each system of linear equations by adding or subtracting. Check your answer.

1. $x - 5y = 10$
    $2x + 5y = 5$

    _____

2. $x + y = -10$
    $5x + y = -2$

    _____

3. $4x + 10y = 2$
    $-4x + 8y = 16$

    _____

4. $-3x - 7y = 8$
    $3x - 2y = -44$

    _____

5. $-x + 4y = 15$
    $3x + 4y = 3$

    _____

6. $-4x + 11y = 5$
    $4x - 11y = -5$

    _____

7. $-x - y = 1$
    $-x + y = -1$

    _____

8. $3x - 5y = 60$
    $4x + 5y = -4$

    _____

Write a system of equations to solve.

9. A plumber charges an initial amount to make a house call plus an hourly rate for the time he is working. A 1-hour job costs $90 and a 3-hour job costs $210. What is the initial amount and the hourly rate that the plumber charges?

    _____

10. A man and his three children spent $40 to attend a show. A second family of three children and their two parents spent $53 for the same show. How much does a child's ticket cost?

    _____

Solving Linear Systems by Adding or Subtracting

LESSON 11-3

Practice and Problem Solving: C

Solve each system of linear equations by adding or subtracting. Check your answer.

1. $0.5x - 3y = 1$
   $1.5x + 3y = 9$

2. $2x + \dfrac{1}{2}y = 6$

   $2x + \dfrac{1}{4}y = 8$

_____   _____

3. $-4x + 7y = 11$
   $4x - 9y = -13$

4. $\dfrac{1}{3}x + y = 0$

   $\dfrac{2}{5}x + y = 5$

_____   _____

5. A theater charges $25 for adults and $15 for children. When the theater increases its prices next year, the price of a child's ticket will increase to $18 and the cost for the members of a dance club to attend the theater will increase from $450 to $480. Write and solve a system of equations to find how many adults are in the dance club.

_____

6. Pearl solved a system of two linear equations. In the final step, she found herself writing "0 = 6." Pearl thought she had done something wrong, but she had not. Explain what occurred here and how the graphs of the two equations are related.

_____

_____

7. The equations $ax + by = c$ and $dx - by = e$ form a system of equations where a, b, c, d, and e are real numbers with $a \neq -d$. Solve the system for x.

_____

_____

LESSON 11-4

Solving Linear Systems by Multiplying First
Practice and Problem Solving: A/B

Solve each system of equations. Check your answer.

1. $\begin{cases} -3x - 4y = -2 \\ 6x + 4y = 3 \end{cases}$

2. $\begin{cases} 2x - 2y = 14 \\ x + 4y = -13 \end{cases}$

_____

3. $\begin{cases} y - x = 17 \\ 2y + 3x = -11 \end{cases}$

4. $\begin{cases} x + 6y = 1 \\ 2x - 3y = 32 \end{cases}$

_____

5. $\begin{cases} 3x + y = -15 \\ 2x - 3y = 23 \end{cases}$

6. $\begin{cases} 5x - 2y = -48 \\ 2x + 3y = -23 \end{cases}$

_____

Solve each system of equations. Check your answer by graphing.

7. $\begin{cases} 4x - 3y = -9 \\ 5x - y = 8 \end{cases}$

8. $\begin{cases} 3x - 3y = -1 \\ 12x - 2y = 16 \end{cases}$

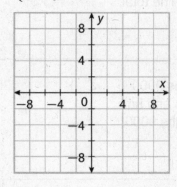
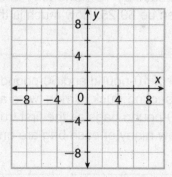

Solve.

9. Ten bagels and four muffins cost $13. Five bagels and eight muffins cost $14. What are the prices of a bagel and a muffin?

_____

10. John can service a television and a cable box in one hour. It took him four hours yesterday to service two televisions and ten cable boxes. How many minutes does John need to service a cable box?

_____

LESSON 11-4

Solving Linear Systems by Multiplying First
Practice and Problem Solving: C

Solve each system of equations. Check your answer.

1. $-x + \dfrac{1}{2}y = 8$

   $3x - 4y = -39$

   _____

2. $\dfrac{1}{3}x + \dfrac{1}{4}y = 5$

   $\dfrac{1}{6}x - \dfrac{2}{3}y = 31$

   _____

3. $5x = 3y + 18$

   $3x + 5y = 4$

   _____

4. $0.25x - 6y = 17$

   $0.07x + 0.4y = -2$

   _____

Write a system of equations to solve.

5. Travis has $60 in dimes and quarters. If he could switch the numbers of dimes with the number of quarters, he would have $87. How many of each coin does Travis have?

   _____

6. The total cost of a bus ride and a ferry ride is $8.00. In one month, bus fare will increase by 10% and ferry fare will increase by 25%. The total cost will then be $9.25. How much is the current bus fare?

   _____

7. A truckload of 10-pound and 50-pound bags of fertilizer weighs 9000 pounds. A second truck carries twice as many 10-pound bags and half as many 50-pound bags as the first truck. That load also weighs 9000 pounds. How many of each bag are on the first truck?

   _____

8. The hundreds digit and the ones digit of a three-digit number are the same. The sum of its three digits is 16. If the tens digit and the ones digit are exchanged, the number increases by 45. What is the number?

   _____

Name _____ Date _____ Class_____

Creating Systems of Linear Equations
Practice and Problem Solving: A/B

Write and solve a system of equations for each situation.

1. One week Beth bought 3 apples and 8 pears for $14.50. The next week she bought 6 apples and 4 pears and paid $14. Find the cost of 1 apple and the cost of 1 pear.

_____

2. Brian bought beverages for his coworkers. One day he bought 3 lemonades and 4 iced teas for $12.00. The next day he bought 5 lemonades and 2 iced teas for $11.50. Find the cost of 1 lemonade and 1 iced tea, to the nearest cent.

_____

Two campgrounds rent a campsite for one night according to the following table. Use the table for 3–5.

Number of campers	Sunnyside Campground	Green Mountain Campground
1	$58	$40
2	$66	$50
3	$74	$60
4	$82	$70

3. Write the equation for the rate charged by Sunnyside Campground.

_____

4. Write the equation for the rate charged by Green Mountain.

_____

5. Solve the system of the equations you found in Problems 3 and 4. For how many campers do the campgrounds charge the same rate? What is the rate charged for that number of campers?

_____

Use the graph for 6–8.

6. Write the functions represented by the graph. _____

7. What does each function represent? What does the variable represent?

_____

8. Solve the system of equations. Is the intersection point shown on the graph correct?

_____

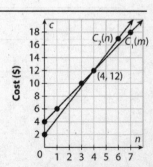

Number of Dogs Walked

LESSON 12-1

Creating Systems of Linear Equations

Practice and Problem Solving: C

Use the graph for 1–3.

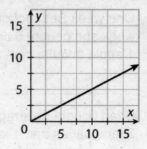

1. Write the equation for the line of the graph.

2. Develop a real-world scenario that could be solved by this equation. Examples may be "the number of bales of hay needed to feed 4 elephants," or "the cost of 6 sandwiches and 4 iced teas." Record your idea:

   _____

   _____

3. Select one point on the line. Write two more equations that also have this point as a solution. Graph the two new equations.

   Let *x* = _____   Let *y* = _____

   equations: _____   _____

4. Make a chart of the information another student could use to write the equations and find the solution for all three equations. What information will you need to show? Label the columns and rows according to the scenario you chose.

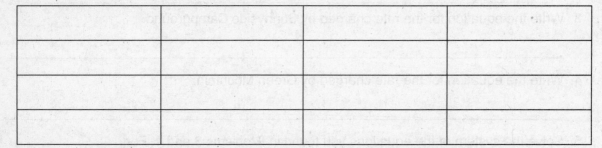

5. Write your own problem, asking students to find the equations from the chart above. Write a complete solution for your problem on another sheet of paper.

   _____

   _____

   _____

LESSON
12-2

Graphing Systems of Linear Inequalities
Practice and Problem Solving: A/B

Tell whether the ordered pair is a solution of the given system.

1. $(2, -2); \begin{cases} y < x - 3 \\ y > -x + 1 \end{cases}$

2. $(2, 5); \begin{cases} y > 2x \\ y \geq x + 2 \end{cases}$

3. $(1, 3); \begin{cases} y \leq x + 2 \\ y > 4x - 1 \end{cases}$

_____ _____ _____

**Graph the system of linear inequalities. a. Give two ordered pairs
that are solutions. b. Give two ordered pairs that are not solutions.**

4. $\begin{cases} y \leq x + 4 \\ y \geq -2x \end{cases}$

5. $\begin{cases} y \leq \dfrac{1}{2}x + 1 \\ x + y < 3 \end{cases}$

6. $\begin{cases} y > x - 4 \\ y < x + 2 \end{cases}$

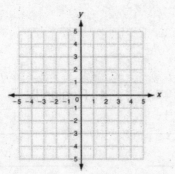 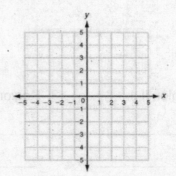 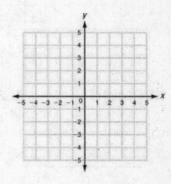

a. _____   a. _____   a. _____

b. _____   b. _____   b. _____

7. Charlene makes $10 per hour babysitting and $5 per hour
gardening. She wants to make at least $80 a week,
but can work no more than 12 hours a week.

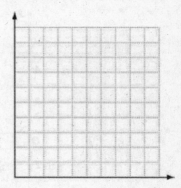

 a. Write a system of linear equations.

 _____

 b. Graph the solutions of the system.

 c. Describe all the possible combinations of hours that
    Charlene could work at each job.

 _____

 _____

 d. List two possible combinations. _____

_____

LESSON
12-2

Graphing Systems of Linear Inequalities

Practice and Problem Solving: C

The coordinate grid below shows a system of two linear equations. For each problem, state the system of inequalities that generates the region indicated as its solution. Write the inequalities in terms of *y*.

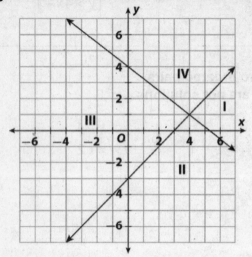

1. Region I

2. Region II

3. Region III

4. Region IV

_____   _____   _____   _____

_____   _____   _____   _____

The inequalities $x \geq -5$, $y \geq -5$, $x + y \leq 1$, and $2x - y \leq 5$ form a system. Use this system for Problems 5–7.

5. Graph the system.

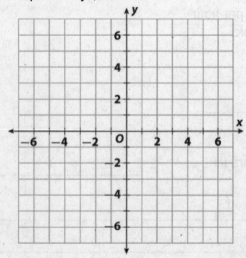

6. Describe geometrically the shaded region that represents the system's solution. Identify the vertices of that region.

7. Each square on the coordinate grid has an area of 1 square unit. Find the area of the shaded region in your graph above. Show your method fully.

Name _____ Date _____ Class_____

 LESSON 12-3

Modeling with Linear Systems
Practice and Problem Solving: A/B

Write a system of equations to solve each problem.

1. For a small party of 12 people, the caterer offered a choice of a steak dinner for $12.00 per meal or a chicken dinner for $10.50 per meal. The final cost for the meals was $138.00. How many of each meal was ordered?

   Equations: _____

   Solution: _____

2. A clubhouse was furnished with a total of 9 couches and love seats so that all 23 members of the club could be seated at once. Each couch seats 3 people and each love seat seats 2 people. How many couches and how many love seats are in the clubhouse?

   Equations: _____

   Solution: _____

3. A small art museum charges $5 for an adult ticket and $3 for a student ticket. At the end of the day, the museum had sold 89 tickets and made $371. How many student tickets and how many adult tickets were sold?

   Equations: _____

   Solution: _____

4. Cassie has a total of 110 coins in her piggy bank. All the coins are quarters and dimes. The coins have a total value of $20.30. How many quarters and how many dimes are in the piggy bank?

   Equations: _____

   Solution: _____

Write a system of inequalities and graph them to solve the problem.

5. Jack is buying tables and chairs for his deck party. Tables cost $25 and chairs cost $15. He plans to spend no more than $285 and buy at least 16 items. Show and describe the solution set, and suggest a reasonable solution to the problem.

   Equations: _____

   Solution: _____

Original content Copyright © by Houghton Mifflin Harcourt. Additions and changes to the original content are the responsibility of the instructor.

81

Modeling with Linear Systems

Practice and Problem Solving: C

Write and solve a system of linear equations for each problem.
Solve each problem using two different methods.

1. A flower shop displays 41 vases for sale throughout
   the shop. Large vases cost $22 each and small
   vases cost $14 each. The vases on display have
   a combined value of $710. How many of each
   size of vase are on display?

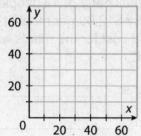

   Equations: _____

   _____

   Solution: _____

2. Some members of the ski club and some
   faculty chaperones are on an overnight ski trip.
   They reserved one $120 hotel room for every
   4 students and one $90 hotel room for every 2
   faculty chaperones, or 27 rooms in all for $2880.
   How many students and how many faculty
   chaperones are on the trip?

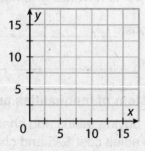

   Equations: _____

   _____

   Solution: _____

Write a system of inequalities and graph them to solve the problem.

3. Lane is buying fish for his aquarium. Tetras
   cost $5 each and cichlids cost $19 each.
   Lane would like to have at least 8 fish in all,
   but he can spend no more than $100.
   Describe the solution set and give a
   reasonable solution.

   Equations: _____

   _____

   Solution set: _____

   Solution: _____

LESSON 13-1

Understanding Piecewise-Defined Functions

Practice and Problem Solving: A/B

Graph each piecewise-defined function.

1. $f(x) = \begin{cases} 0.5x - 1.5 & x < -1 \\ x + 1 & -1 \le x \le 3 \\ 4 & x > 3 \end{cases}$

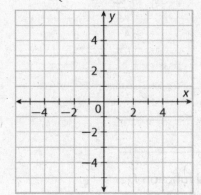

2. $f(x) = \begin{cases} -4x - 16 & x < -3 \\ 0.5x - 4.5 & -3 \le x < 3 \\ -2 & x \ge 3 \end{cases}$

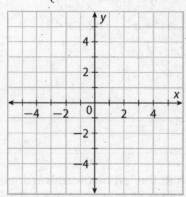

Write equations to complete the definition of each function.

3.

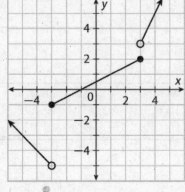

_____

4.

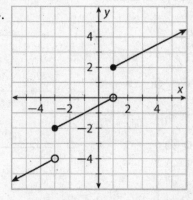

_____

5. The graph at the right shows shipping cost as a function of purchase amount.

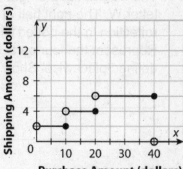

Purchase Amount (dollars)

Find the shipping cost for each purchase amount.

purchase amount: $8.49 _____

purchase amount: $20.00 _____

purchase amount: $89.50 _____

purchase amount: $40.01 _____

LESSON
13-1
Understanding Piecewise-Defined Functions
Practice and Problem Solving: C

1. The incomplete piecewise-defined function at the right is represented by this graph.

   Find real numbers *a* and *c* to complete the definition of *f*. Show your work.

   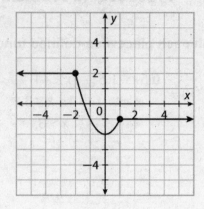

   $$f(x) = \begin{cases} 2 & x < -2 \\ ax^2 + c & -2 \leq x \leq 1 \\ -1 & x > 1 \end{cases}$$

   _____

   _____

   _____

2. The graph at the left below represents a piecewise-defined function *f*. It is defined for all real numbers *x*. The pattern shown continues as suggested both to the left and to the right indefinitely. Which is greater, *f*(48) or *f*(30)? Explain.

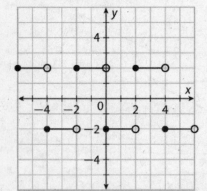

   _____

   _____

   _____

   _____

3. The diagram at the right shows the left half of the letter W. The right half of the letter is formed by reflection in the dotted line.
   Represent the four parts of the letter as a function *f* defined piecewise. Show your work.

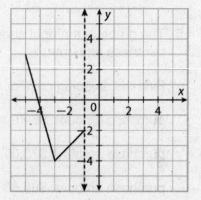

Absolute Value Functions and Transformations

LESSON 13-2

Practice and Problem Solving: A/B

Create a table of values for $f(x)$, graph the function, and tell the domain and range.

1. $f(x) = |x - 3| + 2$

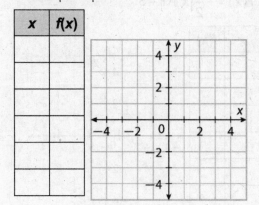

2. $f(x) = 2|x + 1| - 2$

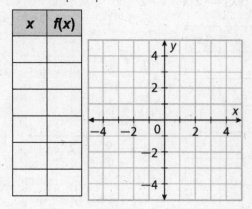

_____   _____

Write an equation for each absolute value function whose graph is shown.

3.

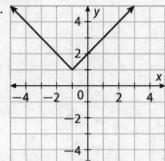

4.

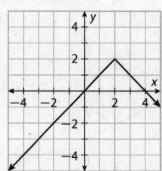

_____   _____

Solve.

5. A machine is used to fill bags with sand. The average weight of a bag filled with sand is 22.3 pounds. Write an absolute value function describing the difference between the weight of an average bag of sand and a bag of sand with an unknown weight.

_____

_____

LESSON 13-2 Absolute Value Functions and Transformations

Practice and Problem Solving: C

Create a table of values for *f(x)*, graph the function, and tell the domain and range.

1. $f(x) = -2|x - 1| + 2$

x	f(x)

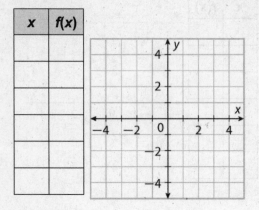

2. $f(x) = -\frac{1}{2}|x + 1| + 3$

x	f(x)

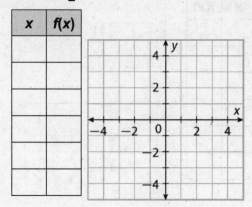

_____

Write an equation for each absolute value function whose graph is shown.

3.

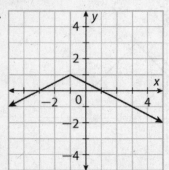

4.

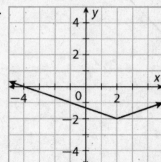

_____   _____

Solve.

5. Suppose you plan to ride your bicycle from Portland, Oregon, to Seattle, Washington, and back to Portland. The distance between Portland and Seattle is 175 miles. You plan to ride 25 miles each day. Write an absolute value function *d(x)*, where *x* is the number of days into the ride, that describes your distance from Portland and use your function to determine the number of days it will take to complete your ride.

_____

LESSON 13-3

Solving Absolute Value Equations

Practice and Problem Solving: A/B

Solve.

1. How many solutions does the equation $|x + 7| = 1$ have? _____

2. How many solutions does the equation $|x + 7| = 0$ have? _____

3. How many solutions does the equation $|x + 7| = -1$ have? _____

Solve each equation algebraically.

4. $|x| = 12$

5. $|x| = \dfrac{1}{2}$

6. $|x| - 6 = 4$

_____   _____   _____

7. $5 + |x| = 14$

8. $3|x| = 24$

9. $|x + 3| = 10$

_____   _____   _____

Solve each equation graphically.

10. $|x - 1| = 2$

11. $4|x - 5| = 12$

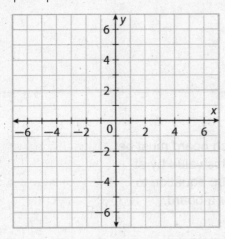 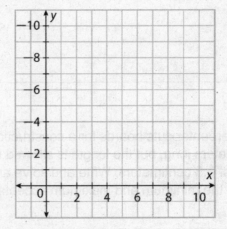

_____   _____

Leticia sets the thermostat in her apartment to 68 degrees. The actual temperature in her apartment can vary from this by as much as 3.5 degrees.

12. Write an absolute-value equation that you can

   use to find the minimum and maximum temperature. _____

13. Solve the equation to find the minimum and

   maximum temperature. _____

LESSON 13-3 Solving Absolute Value Equations

Practice and Problem Solving: C

Solve each equation algebraically.

1. $|x| + 6 = -4$

_____

2. $-9|x| = -63$

3. $|x + 11| = 0$

4. $\left|x - \dfrac{1}{2}\right| = 2$

_____

5. $3|x - 1| = -15$

6. $|x - 1| - 1.4 = 6.2$

Solve each equation graphically.

7. $\dfrac{|4x - 1|}{2} = 1$

8. $-3|5x - 2| = -12$

_____   _____

Solve.

9. A carpenter cuts boards for a construction project. Each board must be 3 meters long, but the length is allowed to differ from this value by at most 0.5 centimeters. Write and solve an absolute-value equation to find the minimum and maximum acceptable lengths for a board.

_____

_____

10. The owner of a butcher shop keeps the shop's freezer at –5 °C. It is acceptable for the temperature to differ from this value by 1.5 °C. Write and solve an absolute-value equation to find the minimum and maximum acceptable temperatures.

_____

_____

LESSON 13-4

Solving Absolute Value Inequalities

Practice and Problem Solving: A/B

Solve each inequality and graph the solutions.

1. $|x| - 2 \le 3$

   _____

   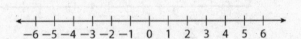

2. $|x + 1| + 5 < 7$

   _____

   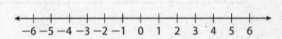

3. $3|x - 6| \le 9$

   _____

   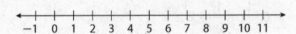

4. $|x + 3| - 1.5 < 2.5$

   _____

   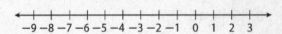

5. $|x| + 17 > 20$

   _____

   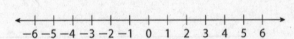

6. $|x - 6| - 7 > -3$

   _____

   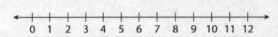

7. $\frac{1}{2}|x + 5| \ge 2$

   _____

   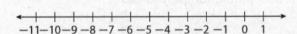

8. $2|x - 2| \ge 3$

   _____

   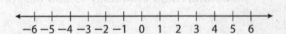

Solve.

9. The organizers of a drama club wanted to sell 350 tickets to their show. The actual sales were no more than 35 tickets from this goal. Write and solve an absolute-value inequality to find the range of the number of tickets that could have been sold.

   _____

10. The temperature at noon in Los Angeles on a summer day was 88 °F. During the day, the temperature varied from this by as much as 7.5 °F. Write and solve an absolute-value inequality to find the range of possible temperatures for that day.

   _____

   _____

LESSON 13-4

Solving Absolute Value Inequalities

Practice and Problem Solving: C

Solve each inequality and graph the solutions.

1. $|x| - 7 < -4$

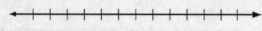

2. $|x - 3| + 0.7 < 2.7$

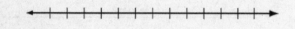

3. $\frac{1}{3}|x + 2| \leq 1$

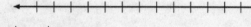

4. $|x - 5| - 3 > 1$

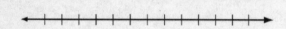

5. $|5x| \geq 15$

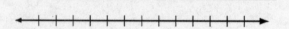

6. $\left|x + \frac{1}{2}\right| - 2 \geq 2$

7. $|x - 2| + 7 \geq 3$

8. $4|x - 6| \geq -8$

Solve.

9. The ideal temperature for a refrigerator is 36.5 °F. It is acceptable for the temperature to differ from this value by at most 1.5 °F. Write and solve an absolute-value inequality to find the range of acceptable temperatures.

10. At a trout farm, most of the trout have a length of 23.5 cm. The length of some of the trout differs from this by as much as 2.1 cm. Write and solve an absolute-value inequality to find the range of lengths of the trout.

11. Ben says that there is no solution for this absolute-value inequality. Is he correct? If not, solve the inequality. Explain how you know you are correct.

$$32 + \frac{|x - 7|}{13} < 7$$

LESSON 14-1 Understanding Geometric Sequences

Practice and Problem Solving: A/B

Find the common ratio *r* for each geometric sequence and use *r* to find the next three terms.

1. 3, 9, 27, 81, ...   *r* = _____

   Next three terms: _____

2. 972, 324, 108, 36, ...   *r* = _____

   Next three terms: _____

Complete.

3. The 11th term in a geometric sequence is 48 and the common ratio is 4.

   The 12th term is _____ and the 10th term is _____.

4. 7 and 105 are successive terms in a geometric sequence. The

   term following 105 is _____ .

Find the common difference *d* of the arithmetic sequence and write the next three terms.

5. 6, 11, 16, 21, ...   *d* = _____

   Next three terms: _____

6. 7, 4, 1, –2, ...   *d* = _____

   Next three terms: _____

Use the table to answer Exercise 7.

Bounce	Height
1	24
2	12
3	6

7. A ball is dropped from the top of a building.

   The table shows its height in feet above ground at the top of each bounce.

   What is the height of the ball at the top of bounce 5? _____

8. Tom's bank balances at the end of months 1, 2, and 3 are $1600,

   $1664, and $1730.56. What will Tom's balance be at the end of month 5? _____

9. Consider the geometric sequence 6, –18, 54.... Select all that apply.

   - A. The common ratio is 3.
   - B. The 6th term is –1458.
   - C. The 4th term is –3 times 54.
   - D. $6(-3)^{11}$ is smaller than $6(-3)^{10}$.

Find the indicated term by using the common ratio.

10. 108, –72, 48, ...; 5th term

    _____

Understanding Geometric Sequences
Practice and Problem Solving: C

Find the common ratio *r* for each geometric sequence and use *r* to find the next three terms.

1. 4, 5, 6.25, ... $r = $ _____

   Next three terms: _____

2. 864, –288, 96, ... $r = $ _____

   Next three terms: _____

Complete.

3. The 11th term in a geometric sequence is 48 and the common ratio is –0.8.

   The 12th term is _____ and the 10th term is _____.

4. 8.5 and 11.9 are successive terms in a geometric sequence. The

   term following 11.9 is _____ .

Find the common difference *d* of the arithmetic sequence and write the next three terms.

5. 8, 17.6, 27.2, ... $d = $ _____

   Next three terms: _____

6. 4, –2.5, –9, ... $d = $ _____

   Next three terms: _____

Use the table to answer Exercise 7.

Bounce	Height
1	36
2	27
3	20.25

7. A ball is dropped from the top of a building.

   The table shows its height in feet above ground at the top of each bounce.

   To the nearest hundredth, what is the height of the ball at the top of bounce 5?

8. Lee's bank balances at the end of months 1, 2, and 3 are $1600, $1640, and $1681.

   What will Lee's balance be at the end of month 5? _____

9. Consider the geometric sequence –12, 19.2, –30.72.... Select all that apply.
   - A. The common ratio is –1.6.
   - C. The 4th term is 1.6 times –30.72.
   - B. The 5th term is 78.6432.
   - D. $-12(-1.6)^9$ is smaller than $-12(-1.6)^8$.

Find the indicated term by using the common ratio.

10. 108, –27, 6.75, ...; 5th term

   _____

LESSON 14-2

Constructing Geometric Sequences

Practice and Problem Solving: A/B

Complete.

1. Below are the first five terms of a geometric series. Fill in the bottom row by writing each term as the product of the first term and a power of the common ratio.

N	1	2	3	4	5
f(n)	3	12	48	192	768
f(n)					

The general rule is $f(n) =$ _____.

Each rule represents a geometric sequence. If the given rule is recursive, write it as an explicit rule. If the rule is explicit, write it as a recursive rule. Assume that $f(1)$ is the first term of the sequence.

2. $f(n) = 11(2)^{n-1}$

3. $f(1) = 2.5; f(n) = f(n-1) \cdot 3.5$ for $n \geq 2$

_____

_____

4. $f(1) = 27; f(n) = f(n-1) \cdot \dfrac{1}{3}$ for $n \geq 2$

5. $f(n) = -4(0.5)^{n-1}$

_____

_____

Write an explicit rule for each geometric sequence based on the given terms from the sequence. Assume that the common ratio r is positive.

6. $a_1 = 90$ and $a_2 = 360$

7. $a_1 = 16$ and $a_3 = 4$

_____

_____

8. $a_1 = 2$ and $a_5 = 162$

9. $a_2 = 30$ and $a_3 = 10$

_____

_____

A bank account earns a constant rate of interest each month. The account was opened on March 1 with $18,000 in it. On April 1, the balance in the account was $18,045. Use this information for 10–12.

10. Write an explicit rule and a recursive rule that can be used to find $A(n)$, the balance after n months.

_____

11. Find the balance after 5 months. _____

12. Find the balance after 5 years. _____

LESSON 14-2

Constructing Geometric Sequences

Practice and Problem Solving: C

Each rule represents a geometric sequence. If the given rule is recursive, write it as an explicit rule. If the rule is explicit, write it as a recursive rule. Assume that $f(1)$ is the first term of the sequence.

1. $f(1) = \dfrac{2}{3}; f(n) = f(n-1) \bullet 8$ for $n \geq 2$

2. $f(n) = -10(0.4)^{n-1}$

_____   _____

Write an explicit rule for each geometric sequence based on the given terms from the sequence. Assume that the common ratio r is positive.

3. $a_1 = 6$ and $a_4 = 162$

4. $a_2 = 9$ and $a_4 = 2.25$

_____   _____

5. $a_4 = 0.01$ and $a_5 = 0.0001$

6. $a_3 = \dfrac{1}{48}$ and $a_4 = \dfrac{1}{192}$

_____   _____

7. $a_3 = 32$ and $a_6 = \dfrac{256}{125}$

8. $a_2 = -4$ and $a_4 = -9$

_____   _____

Solve.

9. A geometric sequence contains the terms $a_3 = 40$ and $a_5 = 640$.
   Write the explicit rules for $r > 0$ and for $r < 0$.

_____

10. The sum of the first n terms of the geometric sequence $f(n) = ar^{n-1}$

    can be found using the formula $\dfrac{a(r^n - 1)}{r-1}$. Use this formula to find the

    sum $1 + 3 + 3^2 + 3^3 + ... + 3^{10}$. Check your answer the long way.

_____

11. An account earning interest compounded annually was worth $44,100 after 2 years and $48,620.25 after 4 years. What is the interest rate?

_____

12. There are 64 teams in a basketball tournament. All teams play in the first round but only winning teams move on to subsequent rounds. Write an explicit rule for $T(n)$, the number of games in the nth round of the tournament. State the domain:

_____

LESSON 14-3

Constructing Exponential Functions
Practice and Problem Solving: A/B

Use two points to write an equation for each function shown.

1.

x	0	1	2	3
f(x)	6	18	54	162

_____

2.

x	−2	0	2	4
f(x)	84	21	5.25	1.3125

_____

Complete the table using domain of {−2, −1, 0, 1, 2} for each function shown. Graph each.

3. $f(x) = 3(2)^x$

x	−2	−1	0	1	2
f(x)					

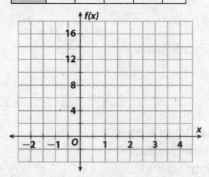

4. $f(x) = 4(0.5)^x$

x	−2	−1	0	1	2
f(x)					

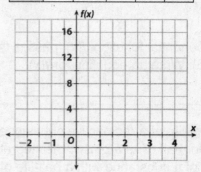

Graph each function.

5. $y = 5(2)^x$

6. $y = -2(3)^x$

7. $y = 3\left(\dfrac{1}{2}\right)^x$

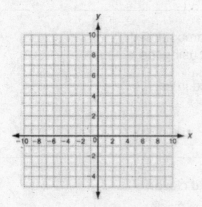
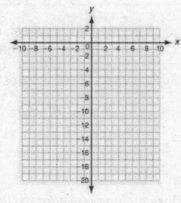
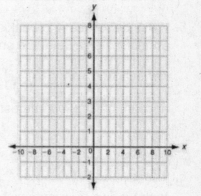

Solve.

8. If a basketball is bounced from a height of 15 feet, the function
   $f(x) = 15(0.75)^x$ gives the height of the ball in feet at each bounce,
   where x is the bounce number. What will be the height of the fifth bounce?

   Round to the nearest tenth of a foot. _____

LESSON 14-3

Constructing Exponential Functions
Practice and Problem Solving: C

Graph each function. On your graph, include points to indicate the ordered pairs for $x = -1, 0, 1,$ and 2.

1. $f(x) = 0.75(2)^x$

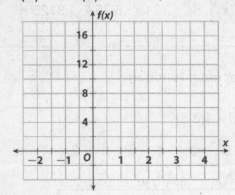

2. $f(x) = 5(4)^{-x}$

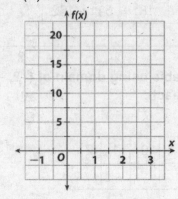

Solve.

3. An exponential function, $f(x)$, passes through the points (2, 360) and (3, 216). Write an equation for $f(x)$.

_____

4. The half-life of a radioactive substance is the average amount of time it takes for half of its atoms to disintegrate. Suppose you started with 200 grams of a substance with a half-life of 3 minutes. How many minutes have passed if 25 grams now remain? Explain your reasoning.

_____

_____

5. If A is deposited in a bank account at $r\%$ annual interest, compounded annually, its value at the end of n years, $V(n)$, can be found using the

formula $V(n) = A\left(1 + \dfrac{r}{100}\right)^n$. Suppose that $5000 is invested in an

account paying 4% interest. Find its value after 10 years.

_____

6. The graph of $f(x) = 5(4)^{-x}$ from Problem 2 moves closer and closer to the x-axis as x increases. Does the graph ever reach the x-axis? Explain your reasoning and what your conclusion implies about the range of the function.

_____

_____

LESSON 14-4

Graphing Exponential Functions

Practice and Problem Solving: A/B

Graph each exponential function. Identify *a*, *b*, the *y*-intercept, and the end behavior of the graph.

1. $f(x) = 4(2)^x$

x	−2	−1	0	1	2
f(x)					

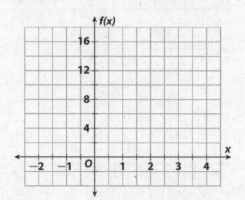

$a = $ ____ $b = $ ____ y-intercept = ____

end behavior: $x \rightarrow -\infty = $ ____ , $x \rightarrow +\infty = $ ____

2. $f(x) = \frac{1}{3}(3)^x$

x	−2	−1	0	1	2
f(x)					

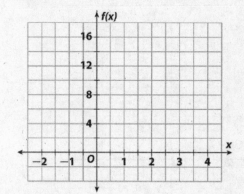

$a = $ ____ $b = $ ____ y-intercept = ____

end behavior: $x \rightarrow -\infty = $ ____ , $x \rightarrow +\infty = $ ____

3. $f(x) = -3(2)^x$

x	−2	−1	0	1	2
f(x)					

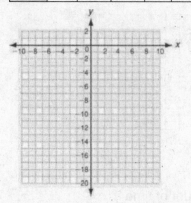

$a = $ ____ $b = $ ____ y-intercept = ____

end behavior: $x \rightarrow -\infty = $ ____ , $x \rightarrow +\infty = $ ____

4. $f(x) = 3\left(\frac{1}{2}\right)^x$

x	−2	−1	0	1	2
f(x)					

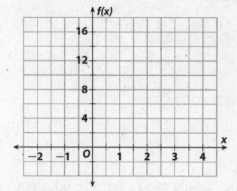

$a = $ ____ $b = $ ____ y-intercept = ____

end behavior: $x \rightarrow -\infty = $ ____ , $x \rightarrow +\infty = $ ____

LESSON 14-4

Graphing Exponential Functions

Practice and Problem Solving: C

Graph each exponential function. Identify *a*, *b*, the *y*-intercept, and the end behavior of the graph.

1. $f(x) = 3.5(2)^x$

x	−2	−1	0	1	2
f(x)					

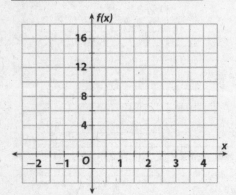

a = ____ *b* = ____ *y*-intercept = ____

end behavior: $x \rightarrow -\infty = $ ____ , $x \rightarrow +\infty = $ ____

2. $f(x) = \frac{1}{2}(3)^x$

x	−2	−1	0	1	2
f(x)					

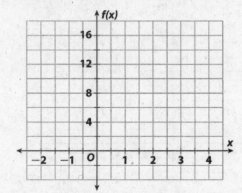

a = ____ *b* = ____ *y*-intercept = ____

end behavior: $x \rightarrow -\infty = $ ____ , $x \rightarrow +\infty = $ ____

Graph each function. On your graph, include points to indicate the ordered pairs for *x* = −1, 0, 1, and 2.

3. $f(x) = -3(2)^x$

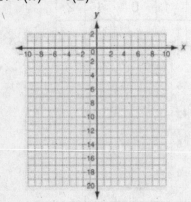

4. $f(x) = 5(4)^{-x}$

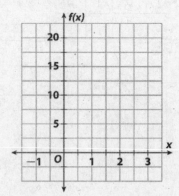

Solve.

5. The half-life of a radioactive substance is the average amount of time it takes for half of its atoms to disintegrate. Suppose you started with 200 grams of a substance with a half-life of 3 minutes. How many minutes have passed if 25 grams now remain? Explain your reasoning.

_____

_____

Transforming Exponential Functions
Practice and Problem Solving: A/B

A parent function has equation $Y_1 = (0.25)^x$. **For 1–4, find the
equation for each** Y_2.

1. Y_2 is a vertical stretch of Y_1. The values of Y_2 are 6 times those of Y_1.

   _____

2. Y_2 is a vertical compression of Y_1. The values of Y_2 are half those of Y_1.

   _____

3. Y_2 is a translation of Y_1 4 units down.

   _____

4. Y_2 is a translation of Y_1 11 units up.

   _____

Values for $f(x)$**, a parent function, and** $g(x)$**, a function in the same
family, are shown below. Use the table for 5–8.**

x	−2	−1	0	1	2
f(x)	0.04	0.2	1	5	25
g(x)	0.016	0.08	0.4	2	10

5. Write equations for the two functions.

   _____

6. Is $g(x)$ a vertical stretch or a vertical compression of $f(x)$? Explain how
   you can tell.

   _____

7. Do the graphs of $f(x)$ and $g(x)$ meet at any points? If so, find where.
   If not, explain why not.

   _____

   _____

8. Let $h(x)$ be the function defined by $h(x) = -f(x)$. Describe how the graph
   of $h(x)$ is related to the graph of $f(x)$.

   _____

   _____

LESSON 14-5

Transforming Exponential Functions

Practice and Problem Solving: C

A parent function has equation $Y_1 = (0.8)^x$. Find the equation for each Y_2, a function created by transforming Y_1.

1. To form Y_2, there is first a vertical stretch of Y_1 such that the values of Y_2 are twice those of Y_1. Then the resulting graph is shifted 8 units up.

   _____

2. To form Y_2, there is first a vertical compression of Y_1 such that the values of Y_2 are one-third those of Y_1. Then the resulting graph is shifted 12 units down.

   _____

3. To form Y_2, the graph of Y_1 is reflected across the *x*-axis.

   _____

4. To form Y_2, the graph of Y_1 is reflected across the *y*-axis.

   _____

5. To form Y_2, the graph of Y_1 is shifted 3 units down and then reflected across the *x*-axis.

   _____

6. To form Y_2, the graph of Y_1 is reflected across the *x*-axis and then shifted 3 units up.

   _____

7. To form Y_2, the graph of Y_1 is shifted 10 units down and then reflected across the *y*-axis.

   _____

8. To form Y_2, the graph of Y_1 is reflected across the *y*-axis and then shifted 10 units down.

   _____

9. To form Y_2, the graph of Y_1 is reflected first across the *x*-axis and then across the *y*-axis.

   _____

10. To form Y_2, the graph of Y_1 is reflected across the *x*-axis, then across the *y*-axis, then across the *x*-axis again, and finally across the *y*-axis.

    _____

LESSON
15-1
Using Graphs and Properties to Solve Equations with Exponents
Practice and Problem Solving: A/B

Solve each equation without graphing.

1. $5^x = 625$

2. $4(2)^x = 128$

3. $\dfrac{6^x}{16} = 81$

_____   _____   _____

4. $\dfrac{1}{12}(6)^x = 108$

5. $\left(\dfrac{4}{5}\right)^x = \dfrac{64}{125}$

6. $\dfrac{2}{3}\left(\dfrac{1}{2}\right)^x = \dfrac{1}{6}$

_____   _____   _____

7. $\dfrac{2}{5}(10)^x = 40$

8. $(0.1)^x = 0.00001$

9. $\dfrac{2}{3}\left(\dfrac{3}{8}\right)^x = \dfrac{9}{256}$

_____   _____   _____

Solve each equation by graphing. Round your answer to the nearest tenth. Write the equations of the functions you graphed first.

10. $9^x = 11$ 11. $12^x = 120$

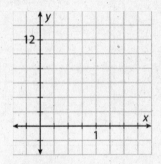   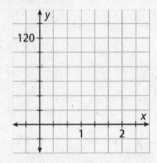

Equation: _____   Equation: _____

Equation: _____   Equation: _____

Solution: _____   Solution: _____

Solve using a graphing calculator. Round your answers to the nearest tenth.

12. A town with a population of 600 is expected to grow at an annual rate of 5%. Write an equation and find the number of years it is expected to take the town to reach a population of 900.

_____

13. How long will it take $20,000 earning 3.5% annual interest to double in value?

_____

LESSON 15-1

Using Graphs and Properties to Solve Equations with Exponents
Practice and Problem Solving: C

Solve each equation without graphing.

1. $\dfrac{1}{27}(3)^x = 9$

2. $\dfrac{5}{16}(2)^x = 160$

3. $\dfrac{25}{27}\left(\dfrac{3}{5}\right)^x = \dfrac{3}{25}$

_____

_____

_____

4. $\dfrac{1}{2}\left(\dfrac{1}{2}\right)^x = \dfrac{1}{2}$

5. $\left(\dfrac{7}{11}\right)^x = \dfrac{11}{7}$

6. $\left(\dfrac{1}{8}\right)^x = 64$

_____

_____

_____

Solve each equation by graphing. Round your answer to the nearest tenth.

7. $(2.72)^x = 3.14$

8. $16(3)^x = 40$

9. $\dfrac{1}{7}\left(\dfrac{7}{8}\right)^x = \dfrac{3}{50}$

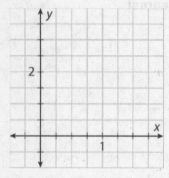

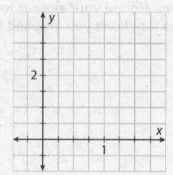

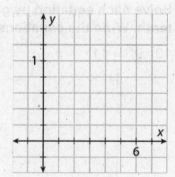

_____

_____

_____

Solve using a graphing calculator.

10. Does $10,000 invested at 6% interest double its value in half the time as $10,000 invested at 3% interest? Show your work.

_____

_____

11. Suppose you were a Revolutionary War veteran and had the foresight to put one penny in a bank account when George Washington became President in 1789. If the bank promised you 5% interest on your account, how much would it be worth in 2014?

_____

_____

LESSON 15-2
Modeling Exponential Growth and Decay
Practice and Problem Solving: A/B

Write an exponential growth function to model each situation. Determine the domain and range of each function. Then find the value of the function after the given amount of time.

1. Annual sales for a fast food restaurant are $650,000 and are increasing at a rate of 4% per year; 5 years _____

_____

2. The population of a school is 800 students and is increasing at a rate of 2% per year; 6 years _____

_____

Write an exponential decay function to model each situation. Determine the domain and range of each function. Then find the value of the function after the given amount of time.

3. The population of a town is 2500 and is decreasing at a rate of 3% per year; 5 years _____

_____

4. The value of a company's equipment is $25,000 and decreases at a rate of 15% per year; 8 years _____

_____

Write an exponential growth or decay function to model each situation. Then graph each function.

5. The population is 20,000 now and expected to grow at an annual rate of 5%.

_____

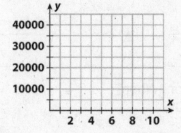

6. A boat that cost $45,000 is depreciating at a rate of 20% per year.

_____

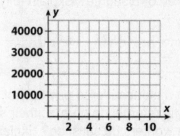

LESSON
15-2

Modeling Exponential Growth and Decay
Practice and Problem Solving: C

Use this information for Problems 1–4.

Odette has two investments that she purchased at the same time.
Investment 1 cost $10,000 and earns 4% interest each year.
Investment 2 cost $8000 and earns 6% interest each year.

1. Write exponential growth functions that could be used to find $v_1(t)$ and $v_2(t)$, the values of the investments after t years.

   _____

2. Find the value of each investment after 5 years. Explain why the difference between their values, which was initially $2000, is now significantly less.

   _____

   _____

3. Will the value of Investment 2 ever exceed the value of Investment 1? If not, why not? If so, when?

   _____

   _____

4. Instead of calculating 4% interest for one year, suppose the interest for Investment 1 was calculated every day at a rate of (4/365)%. This is called daily compounding. Would Odette earn more, the same, or less using this daily method for one year? Provide an example to show your thinking.

   _____

   _____

Solve.

5. A car depreciates in value by 20% each year. Graham argued that the value of the car after 5 years must be $0, since 20% × 5 = 100%. Do you agree or disagree? Explain fully.

   _____

   _____

6. Workers at a plant suffered pay cuts of 10% during a recession. When the economy returned to normal, their salaries were raised 10%. Should the workers be satisfied? Explain your thinking.

   _____

   _____

Name _____ Date _____ Class_____

Using Exponential Regression Models
Practice and Problem Solving: A/B

The table below shows the total attendance at major league baseball games, at 10-year intervals since 1930. Use the table for the problems that follow.

Major League Baseball Total Attendance (y_d), in millions, vs. Years Since 1930 (x)									
x	0	10	20	30	40	50	60	70	80
y_d	10.1	9.8	17.5	19.9	28.7	43.0	54.8	72.6	73.1
y_m									
residual									

1. Use a graphing calculator to find the exponential regression equation for this data. Round a and b to the nearest thousandth.

   _____

2. According to the regression equation, by what percent is attendance growing each year?

   _____

3. Complete the row labeled y_m above. This row contains the predicted y-values for each x-value. Round your answers to the nearest tenth.

4. Calculate the row of residuals above.

5. Analyze the residuals from your table. Does it seem like the equation is a good fit for the data?

   _____

   _____

6. Use your graphing calculator to find the correlation coefficient for the equation and write it below. Does the correlation coefficient make it seem like the equation is a good fit for the data?

   _____

   _____

7. Use the exponential regression equation to predict major league baseball attendance in 2020. Based on your earlier work on this page, do you think this is a reasonable prediction? Explain.

   _____

   _____

Name _____ Date _____ Class _____

Using Exponential Regression Models

LESSON 15-3

Practice and Problem Solving: C

A pot of boiling water is allowed to cool for 50 minutes. The table below shows the temperature of the water as it cools. Use the table for the problems that follow.

Temperature of Water (y_d), in degrees Celsius, after cooling for x minutes											
x	0	5	10	15	20	25	30	35	40	45	50
y_d	100	75	57	44	34	26	21	17	14	11	10
y_m											
residual											

1. Use a graphing calculator to find the exponential regression equation for this data. Round a and b to the nearest thousandth.

_____

2. Complete the rows labeled y_m (predicted y-values) and residual above. Round your answers to the nearest tenth.

3. Fit a linear regression equation to the original data. Write the equation here.

_____

4. The data for the scatter plot is shown in the first two rows of the table below. Complete the next two rows of the table for the model you found in Problem 3.

Temperature of Water (y_d), in degrees Celsius, after cooling for x minutes											
x	0	5	10	15	20	25	30	35	40	45	50
y_d	100	75	57	44	34	26	21	17	14	11	10
y_m											
residual											

5. Examine the residuals in each table. Which appears to be the better model—the linear or exponential equation? Explain.

_____

_____

6. Find the correlation coefficients for the two equations. Based on that information, which equation is the better model? Explain.

_____

Name _____ Date _____ Class_____

Comparing Linear and Exponential Models
Practice and Problem Solving: A/B

Without graphing, tell whether each quantity is changing at a constant amount per unit interval, at a constant percent per unit interval, or neither. Justify your reasoning.

1. A bank account started with $1000 and earned $10 interest per month for two years. The bank then paid 2% interest on the account for the next two years.

   _____

2. Jin Lu earns a bonus for each sale she makes. She earns $100 for the first sale, $150 for the second sale, $200 for the third sale, and so on.

   _____

Use this information for Problems 3–8.

A bank offers annual rates of 6% simple interest or 5% compound interest on its savings accounts. Suppose you have $10,000 to invest.

3. Express $f(x)$, the value of your deposit after x years in the simple interest account, and $g(x)$, the value of your deposit after x years in the compound interest account.

   _____

4. Is either $f(x)$ or $g(x)$ a linear function? An exponential function? How can you tell?

   _____

5. Find the values of your deposit after three years in each account. After three years, which account is the better choice?

   _____

6. Find the values of your deposit after 20 years in each account. After 20 years, which account is the better choice?

   _____

7. Use a graphing calculator to determine the length of time an account must be held for the two choices to be equally attractive. Round your answer to the nearest tenth.

   _____

8. Use your answer to Problem 7 to write a statement that advises an investor regarding how to choose between the two accounts.

   _____

Comparing Linear and Exponential Models
Practice and Problem Solving: C

Without graphing, tell whether each quantity is changing at a constant amount per unit interval, at a constant percent per unit interval, or neither. Justify your reasoning.

1. When Josh read his first book alone, his mother gave him a penny. For his second book, she gave him two cents, and for his third book, she gave him four cents. She plans on doubling the amount for each book Josh reads.

   _____

2. The annual cost of a club membership starts at $100 and increases by $15 each year.

   _____

Use this information for Problems 3–7.

A bank offers annual rates of 4% simple interest or 3.5% compound interest on its savings accounts.

3. Express the values of an initial investment of *A* dollars after *x* years. Let *f*(*x*) represent the amount in a simple interest account and let *g*(*x*) represent the amount in a compound interest account.

   _____

4. If you planned on depositing money for three years, which rate would be a better choice? Explain.

   _____

   _____

5. If you planned on depositing money for 15 years, which rate would be a better choice? Explain.

   _____

   _____

6. Determine the length of time an account must be held for the two choices to be equally attractive. (HINT: You may want to graph the equations.) Round to the nearest tenth.

   _____

7. Would the amount deposited affect any of the answers you gave for Problems 4–6? Justify your reasoning.

   _____

LESSON
16-1
Segment Length and Midpoints
Practice and Problem Solving: A/B

Use a straightedge and a compass to construct a segment of length
AB + *CD*.

1.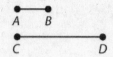

2.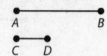

Use the distance formula to determine whether each pair of segments
have the same length.

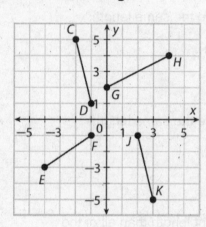

3. $\overline{CD}$ and $\overline{EF}$

4. $\overline{GH}$ and $\overline{JK}$

Determine the coordinates of the midpoint for each segment. Identify
the quadrant that each midpoint lies in.

5. $\overline{PQ}$ has endpoints *P*(5, –3) and *Q*(2, 4).

6. $\overline{RS}$ has endpoints *R*(–2, 3) and *S*(–8, –2).

Midpoint: _____

Midpoint: _____

Quadrant: _____

Quadrant: _____

LESSON 16-1

Segment Length and Midpoints

Practice and Problem Solving: C

Use a straightedge and a compass to construct a segment that has the given length.

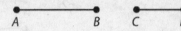

1. $AB + 2(CD)$

2. $2(AB) - CD$

Answer the following questions about the lengths of the segments on the grid. Use the distance formula to justify each answer.

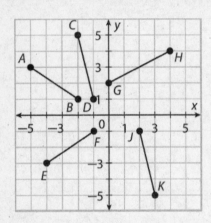

3. $\overline{CD}$ and _____ have the same length.

4. $\overline{EF}$ and _____ have the same length.

5. _____ has a different length than all of the other segments on the grid.

Given triangle *ABC,* determine the coordinates of the vertices of a new triangle formed by the midpoints of each side of triangle *ABC.*

6. $A(-1, -3)$, $B(4, -1)$, $C(3, 4)$

7. $A(4, -4)$, $B(0, 4)$, $C(-3, -1)$

$M_{\overline{AB}}$ (_____, _____)

$M_{\overline{AB}}$ (_____, _____)

$M_{\overline{BC}}$ (_____, _____)

$M_{\overline{BC}}$ (_____, _____)

$M_{\overline{CA}}$ (_____, _____)

$M_{\overline{CA}}$ (_____, _____)

LESSON
16-2

Angle Measures and Angle Bisectors

Practice and Problem Solving: A/B

Construct a copy of each angle.

1.

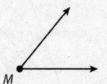

2.

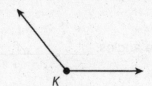

Use a compass and a straightedge to construct the bisector of each angle.

3.

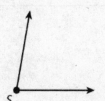

4.

5.

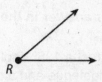

6. Explain how you can use a straightedge and a protractor to show that each angle you formed by a bisector is one-half the original angle.

_____

_____

Determine the measure of each angle. Then describe each angle as acute, right, obtuse, or straight.

7.

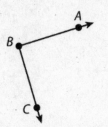

m∠ABC = _____

_____

8.

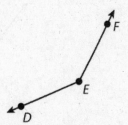

m∠DEF = _____

_____

9.

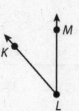

m∠KLM = _____

_____

LESSON 16-2

Angle Measures and Angle Bisectors

Practice and Problem Solving: C

Use the figure for Problems 1–3.

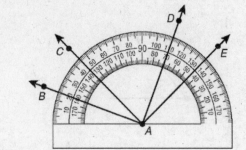

1. Name the obtuse angle. _____

2. Name two acute angles. _____

3. Name two right angles. _____

4. Keisha has a straightedge and a compass, but no protractor. What kind of angle can Keisha draw exactly with only these tools?

_____

Draw your answer in the space provided.

5. Construct a 135° angle using only a straightedge and a compass.

6. An acute angle measures $(6x - 45)°$. Write an inequality to describe the range of all possible values of *x*.   _____

Use only a compass, a straightedge, and the angle shown to construct an angle with the new measure that is given.

7. 21°

8. 32°

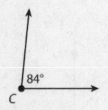

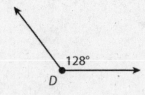

9. $\overrightarrow{DF}$ bisects $\angle CDE$, $\overrightarrow{DG}$ bisects $\angle FDE$, and $\angle CDG = 51°$. Find

m$\angle CDE$. _____

10. m$\angle XWY$ is twice $\angle XWZ$. Explain whether $\overrightarrow{WZ}$ must be the angle bisector of $\angle XWZ$.

LESSON 16-3

Representing and Describing Transformations

Practice and Problem Solving: A/B

1. Use coordinate notation to describe the transformation of △PQR.

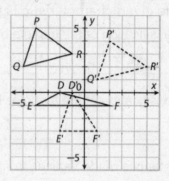

$P(-4, 5)$ → $P'($ _____, _____ $)$

$Q(-5, 2)$ → $Q'($ _____, _____ $)$

$R(-1, 3)$ → $R'($ _____, _____ $)$

2. Describe the algebraic rule for △DEF.

(x, y) → $($ _____, _____ $)$

Name the transformation described by the given rule.

3. (x, y) → $(-x, y)$

_____

4. $(6, 2)$ → $(-6, -2)$

_____

5. $(5, 8)$ → $(8, -5)$

_____

6. (x, y) → $(x + 9, y + 2)$

_____

Draw the image of each figure under the given transformation.

7. (x, y) → $(x + 4, y - 5)$

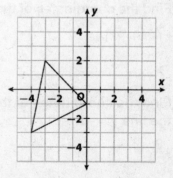

8. A 180° rotation around the origin

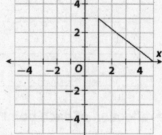

9. A reflection across the *y*-axis

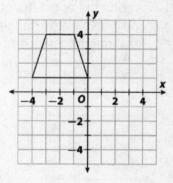

Name _____ Date _____ Class_____

Representing and Describing Transformations
Practice and Problem Solving: C

A triangle undergoes a rigid motion on a coordinate plane. Tell whether the given characteristic is preserved. Write Yes or No.

1. The classification of the triangle by angles (obtuse, etc.)

   _____

2. The classification of the triangles by sides (scalene, etc.)

   _____

3. The distances of the vertices from the origin.

   _____

4. The orientation of the triangle with respect to the coordinate axes.

   _____

5. The area of the triangle

   _____

6. Triangle *A* has been mapped to Triangle *B* through a 180° rotation around the origin. Identify two other series of transformations that could also map Triangle *A* to Triangle *B*. Each series must include at least one translation and at least one reflection, but no rotations.

    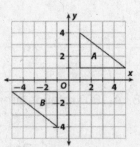

   _____

   _____

   _____

Find the coordinates of the reflection of each point across the line $x = 2$.

7. (5, 3)

   _____

8. (x, y)

   _____

Find the coordinates of the reflection of each point across the line $y = -5$.

9. (3, 4)

   _____

10. (x, y)

   _____

Reasoning and Proof

Practice and Problem Solving: A/B

Write a justification for each step. Choose from the following reasons.

Addition Property of Equality   Division Property of Equality

Segment Addition Postulate   Simplify

Substitution Property of Equality   Subtraction Property of Equality

1.

$HJ = HI + IJ$ _____

$7x - 3 = (2x + 6) + (3x - 3)$ _____

$7x - 3 = 5x + 3$ _____

$7x = 5x + 6$ _____

$2x = 6$ _____

$x = 3$ _____

Show that each conjecture is false by finding a counterexample.

2. For any integer n, $n^3 > 0$. _____

3. Each angle in a right triangle has a different measure.

_____

Make a conjecture about each pattern. Then write the next two items.

4. 1, 2, 2, 4, 8, 32, . . .

_____

_____

5.  ,...

_____

_____

LESSON 16-4

Reasoning and Proof

Practice and Problem Solving: C

Solve. Write justifications for each step in your solution.

1. Solve for $m\angle 3$ in terms of $m\angle 1$. Write justifications for each step in your solution.

   Given: $\angle 1$ and $\angle 2$ are complementary.

   $\angle 2$ and $\angle 3$ are supplementary.

   _____   _____

   _____   _____

   _____   _____

   _____   _____

2. Explain logically how the Transitive Property of Equality can be derived from the Substitution Property of Equality and the Symmetric Property of Equality.

   _____

   _____

   _____

   _____

Make a conjecture about each pattern. Write the next two items.

3. $-1, -8, -27, -64, \ldots$

   _____

4. $1, 11, 21, 1211, 111221, \ldots$ (*Hint:* Try reading the numbers aloud in different ways.)

   _____

Determine if each conjecture is true. If not, write a counterexample.

5. If $a > b$ and $b > c$, then $a - b < a - c$.   _____

6. If n is an integer ($n \neq 0$), then $\dfrac{1}{n} > \left(\dfrac{1}{n}\right)^3$.   _____

LESSON
17-1

Translations

Practice and Problem Solving: A/B

Use the figure below to answer Problems 1–5.

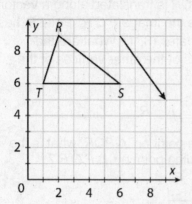

1. Triangle *RST* is translated along vector $\vec{v}$ to create the image *R'S'T'*. What are the coordinates of the vertices of the image?

   R'_____

   S'_____

   T'_____

2. What is the length of vector $\vec{v}$? What is the length of $\overline{RR'}$?

   _____ units   _____ units

3. If (*x*, *y*) is a point on △*RST*, what is the corresponding point on

   △*R'S'T'*? _____

4. Name vector $\vec{v}$ using component form. ⟨___, ___⟩

5. Name a pair of parallel segments formed by vertices of the preimage

   and the image. _____ and _____

Use the figure below to answer Problems 6–8.

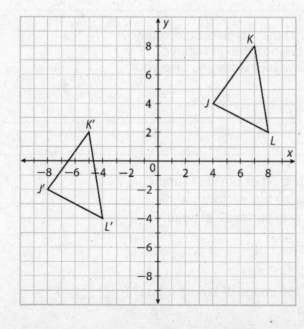

6. Triangle *J'K'L'* is the image of △*JKL* under a translation. Draw the translation vector $\vec{v}$ from *J* to its image in △*J'K'L'*. Write the vector in

   component form. ⟨___, ___⟩

7. What is the slope of $\vec{v}$? _____

8. Triangle *J'K'L'* is also the image of △*DEF* under a translation along a vector ⟨–6, 4⟩. Find the coordinates of points *D*, *E*, and *F*, and draw △*DEF*.

   D _____

   E _____

   F _____

LESSON 17-1

Translations

Practice and Problem Solving: C

Use the figure below to answer Problems 1–9.

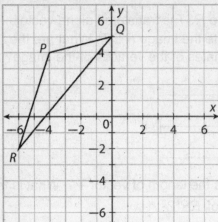

1. Triangle *PQR* is translated along a vector $\bar{v}$ to create the image *P'Q'R'*. Point *P'* has the coordinates (3, 1). What are the coordinates of the other vertices of the image?

   Q' _____ *R'* _____

2. If (*x*, *y*) is a point on △*PQR*, what is the corresponding point on △*P'Q'R'*?

   _____

3. Name vector $\bar{v}$ using component form.

   ⟨___ , ___⟩

4. Using the coordinates of the endpoints, find the slope of *PP'* and of *QQ'*.

   Slope of *PP'* _____ Slope of *QQ'* _____

5. What do the slopes of *PP'* and *QQ'* tell you about the lines?

   _____

6. What is the length of vector $\bar{v}$ (in radical form)? Explain your answer and show your work.

   _____

7. Suppose you want to translate △*PQR* so that the image is completely inside the fourth quadrant and does not go beyond the grid above. How long can the translation vector be? Show your work and give your answer as an inequality in radical form.

   _____

   _____

8. Plot points *A*(−10, −7) and *B*(−6, −4). Mark two other points, *C* and *D*, to make a rhombus in the third quadrant. Name the vector that will translate the rhombus to the first quadrant, with vertex *C'* at point

   (10, 9). ⟨___ , ___⟩

9. What will be the coordinates of vertex *D'* of the image of the rhombus? (___ , ___)

LESSON 17-2

Reflections

Practice and Problem Solving: A/B

Study the figures on the grid and answer the questions.

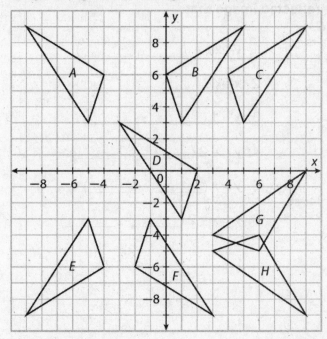

1. Which figure is the reflection of figure *A* over the *y*-axis? _____

2. Which two figures have $x = -3$ as their line of reflection? _____ and _____

3. Which figure is the reflection of figure *A* over the line $y = x$? _____

4. What is the equation of the line of reflection for figures *G* and *H*?

   _____

5. Which figures are **not** reflections of figure *A*? Name all. _____

Use principles of reflections to determine where to place the puck.

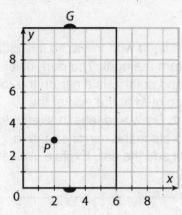

Mike is playing air hockey and wants to bounce the puck off the wall and into the goal at *G*(3, 10).

6. If the puck is at *P* (2, 3), what point on the right wall ($x = 6$) should he aim for? Sketch and label a figure on the grid. Explain your answer.

   _____

   _____

   _____

7. If the puck is at (0, 4), what point on the wall should he aim for?

   (_____ , _____)

8. If the puck is at (3, 2), what point on the wall should he aim for?

   (_____ , _____)

9. If the puck is at (3, 6), what point on the wall should he aim for?

   (_____ , _____)

LESSON 17-2

Reflections

Practice and Problem Solving: C

For each line of symmetry given, make constructions and/or do calculations to find the coordinates in the reflected image that correspond to (x, y) in the preimage, △ABC.

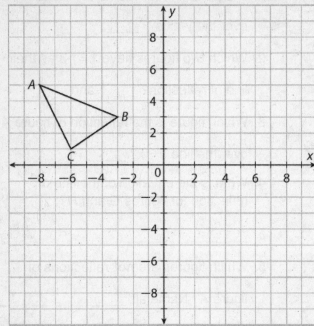

1. y-axis (_____ , _____)

2. x-axis (_____ , _____)

3. x = 1 (_____ , _____)

4. y = − 2 (_____ , _____)

5. y = x (_____ , _____)

6. y = x − 2 (_____ , _____)

Use principles of reflections to solve the problems.

7. The Beckwiths' driveway is lined with trees, so it is difficult to see cars approaching from the right. The dark black line represents the driveway, and point C is a car on the road. A mirror will be placed at point M at the end of the driveway, across the street. Draw and label a sketch to show the angle at which to place the mirror so that a person in the driveway can see the car. Explain your steps.

_____

_____

_____

8. Point P(−2, −3) is reflected across line ℓ. Its image is point Q(8, 12). Find the equation of line ℓ. Describe the steps you took.

y = _____

_____

_____

LESSON
17-3

Rotations

Practice and Problem Solving: A/B

Follow the directions for Problems 1–5 to analyze rotations.

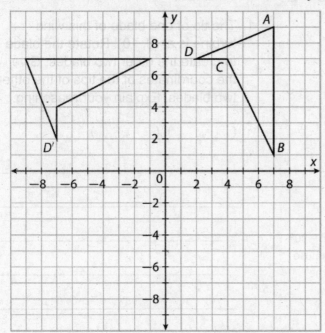

1. Draw a line from the origin, *O*, to point *D* and from *O* to *D'*. Measure the angle formed by $\overline{OD}$ and $\overline{OD}'$. How many degrees was figure

   ABCD rotated? ____ degrees

2. Find the coordinates of points on *ABCD* and corresponding points on its image. Label *A'*, *B'*, and *C'*.

   A(___, ___) A'(___, ___)

   B(___, ___) B'(___, ___)

   C(___, ___) C'(___, ___)

   D(___, ___) D'(___, ___)

   P(x, y) P'(_____ , _____)

3. If you rotate *A'B'C'D'* counterclockwise 90°, what is the sign of the

   x-coordinates of the new image? ____ Of the *y*-coordinates? ____

   In what quadrant is the new image? _____

4. Draw and label *A"B"C"D"*, the image of *A'B'C'D'* after being rotated 90° counterclockwise.

5. If (*x*, *y*) is a point on *ABCD,* what is its image on *A"B"C"D"*?

   (_____, _____)

Use principles of rotations to answer Problems 6–8.

6. What clockwise rotation produces the same image as a counterclockwise rotation of 220°? _____° clockwise

7. Tony Hawk was the first skateboarder to do a "900," a rotation of 900°. How many times did he rotate on the skateboard? _____ times

8. Each arm of this pinwheel is the image of another arm rotated around the center. What is the angle of rotation between one arm and the next? _____°

**LESSON
17-3**

Rotations

Practice and Problem Solving: C

Draw the rotations described in Problems 1–2.

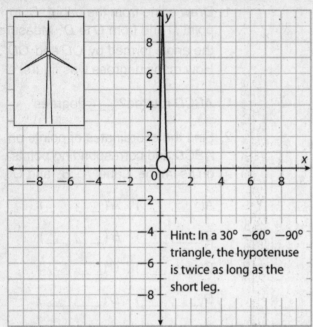

Hint: In a 30° –60° –90° triangle, the hypotenuse is twice as long as the short leg.

1. The tip of one blade of this wind turbine is at (0, 10). Rotate the blade to create the other two blades. Give the coordinates of the tips of the other two blades. Explain your reasoning.

   (___, ___) (___, ___)

   _____

   _____

   _____

   _____

   _____

2. Explain how to draw a rotation of △ABC 45° counterclockwise about point P without using a protractor to measure the angle. Mark the figure to show how to find one point of the image.

   P
   ●

   _____

   _____

Use principles of rotations to answer Problems 3 and 4.

3. A figure in the first quadrant is rotated 180° about the origin. The same figure is reflected over the line $y = -x$. Both transformations produce images in the third quadrant. Under what conditions will the two transformations produce the same image? Explain your answer.

   _____

   _____

   _____

4. The hour hand and minute hand of a clock rotate around the center to show the time. At 12:00 the angle between the hands is 0°. Think about the angles of rotation for each hand during a given time period.

   Find the angle between the hands at 3:40. _____ °

LESSON 17-4

Investigating Symmetry

Practice and Problem Solving: A/B

Use the figures on the grid to answer Problems 1–3.

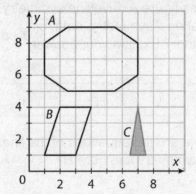

1. What are the equations of the lines of symmetry for figure *A*?

   _____

   _____

2. Does figure *B* have line symmetry, rotational symmetry, or both?

   _____

3. If you rotate figure *C* all the way around point (7, 4), 50° at a time, will you create a figure with rotational symmetry? Explain your answer.

   _____

Tell whether each figure appears to have line symmetry, rotational symmetry, both, or neither. If line symmetry, tell how many lines of symmetry. If rotational symmetry, give the angle of rotational symmetry.

4.   _____

   _____

5.   _____

   _____

6. 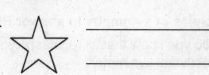   _____

   _____

7. ☆   _____

   _____

Use principles of symmetry to answer Problems 8–9.

8. How many lines of symmetry does each quadrilateral have?

   isosceles trapezoid _____ rectangle with sides 2-4-2-4 _____

   square _____ rhombus _____

   parallelogram with sides 2-4-2-4 and angles ≠ 90° _____

9. How many lines of symmetry does a regular pentagon have? _____

   How many lines of symmetry does a regular hexagon have?_____

Investigating Symmetry

Practice and Problem Solving: C

Use the figures on the grid to answer the questions about symmetry.

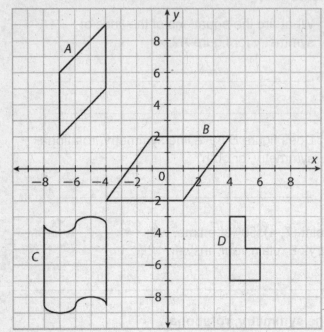

1. Does figure *A* have line symmetry, rotational symmetry, both, or neither? Explain your answer.

   _____

   _____

2. What are the equations of the lines of symmetry for figure *B*?

   y = _____   *y* = _____

3. What do the slopes of the lines tell you?

   _____

   _____

4. Describe the symmetry of figure *C*. _____

5. Describe a series of transformations that you could perform on figure *D* so that the figure and its image form a figure with rotational symmetry.

   _____

Use principles of symmetry to answer Problems 6–8.

6. How do you know that all regular polygons have both line symmetry and rotational symmetry?

   _____

7. If a rotation of 40° will map a symmetrical figure to itself, what other rotations will map the figure to itself? Name all up to 360°.

   _____

8. Name eight angle measures that can be angles of rotational symmetry.

   _____°, _____°, _____°, _____°, _____°, _____°, _____°, _____°.

   What characteristic do all angles of rotational symmetry have in common? Be specific.

   _____

LESSON 18-1

Sequences of Transformations
Practice and Problem Solving: A/B

Draw the image of △ABC after the given combination of transformations.

1. Translation along $\vec{V}$, then reflection across line ℓ

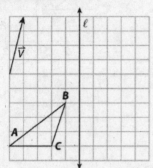

2. 180° rotation around point P, then translation along W

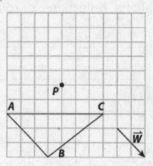

Rectangle ABCD is reflected across the y-axis, rotated 90° clockwise, and translated along the vector ⟨−6, 2⟩. Describe the effect on the figure.

3. Predict the effect of the first transformation.

_____

_____

_____

4. Predict the effect of the second transformation.

_____

_____

_____

_____

5. Predict the effect of the third transformation.

_____

_____

_____

LESSON
18-1

Sequences of Transformations

Practice and Problem Solving: C

Solve.

1. Describe a sequence of three transformations that will result in a mapping of △ABC onto itself. Your sequence must include at least two different types of transformations (translations, reflections, or rotations).

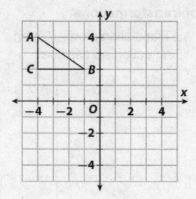

_____

_____

_____

_____

2. △EFG has vertices E(1, 5), F(0, −3), and G(−1, 2). △EFG is translated along the vector ⟨7,1⟩, and the image is reflected across the x-axis. What are the coordinates of the final image of G?

_____

3. △KLM with vertices K(8, −1), L(−1, −4), and M(2, 3) is rotated 180° around the origin. The image is then translated. The final image of K has coordinates (−2, −3). What is the translation vector?

_____

4. Point P has coordinates (a, b). Find the coordinates of P', the image of P after a counterclockwise rotation of 90° around the origin, followed by reflection across the x-axis.

_____

5. Point Q has coordinates (m, n). Find the coordinates of Q', the image of Q after a rotation of 180° around the origin, followed by translation along the vector ⟨g, h⟩.

_____

6. Describe a sequence of three transformations that will result in a mapping of rhombus ABCD onto rhombus A'B'C'D'. Your sequence must include one translation, one reflection, and one rotation.

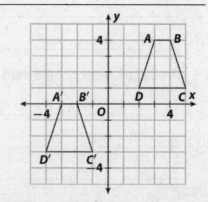

_____

_____

_____

LESSON 18-2

Proving Figures are Congruent Using Rigid Motions

Practice and Problem Solving: A/B

Determine whether △ABC and △MNP are congruent. Explain your answer.

1.
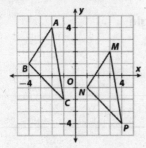

_____

_____

_____

2.
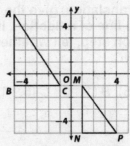

_____

_____

_____

For each pair of congruent figures, specify a sequence of rigid motions that maps one figure onto the other.

3.
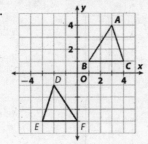

_____

_____

4.
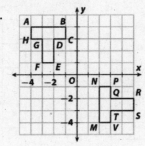

_____

_____

Decide if the angles or the segments in each pair are congruent. Write Yes or No.

5. ∠Q and ∠R

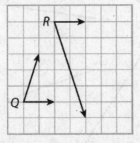

_____

6. $\overline{AB}$ and $\overline{CD}$

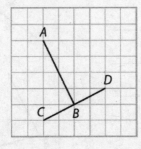

_____

7. $\overline{EF}$ and $\overline{GH}$

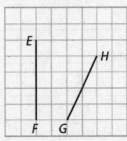

_____

8. ∠S and ∠T

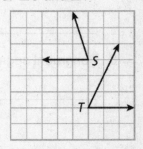

_____

Name _____ Date _____ Class_____

LESSON
18-2

Proving Figures are Congruent Using Rigid Motions
Practice and Problem Solving: C

△*ABC,* with vertices *A*(1, 5), *B*(1, 2), and *C*(6, 1), is transformed in three steps. Describe each step as a translation, reflection, or rotation. If it is a translation, give the translation vector. If it is a reflection, give the line of reflection. If it is a rotation, give the angle of rotation. For each step, tell whether the transformed figure is congruent to △*ABC.*

1. **Step 1:** *A'*(1, −5), *B'*(1, −2), *C'*(6, −1)

   _____

2. **Step 2:** *A"*(−1, 5), *B"*(−1, 2), *C"*(−6, 1)

   _____

3. **Step 3:** *A'''*(2, −1), *B'''*(2, −4), *C'''*(−3, −5)

   _____

Describe the transformation or transformations of the top figure that will produce the image below it.

4.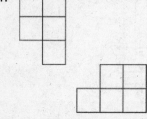

   _____

5.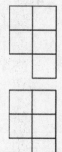

   _____

6.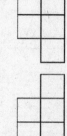

   _____

Identify the congruent pairs on the grid. Describe a series of transformations to prove each answer.

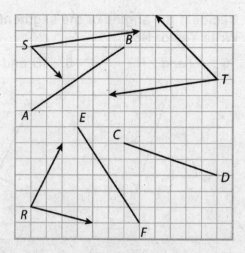

7. Congruent angles: _____

   _____

8. Congruent segments: _____

   _____

LESSON 18-3

Corresponding Parts of Congruent Figures are Congruent

Practice and Problem Solving: A/B

List all of the pairs of congruent angles and sides of the figures.

1. $\triangle KLM \cong \triangle GHI$

_____ $\cong$ _____   _____ $\cong$ _____

_____ $\cong$ _____   _____ $\cong$ _____

_____ $\cong$ _____   _____ $\cong$ _____

2. Rhombus $WXYZ \cong$ rhombus $DEFG$

_____ $\cong$ _____   _____ $\cong$ _____

_____ $\cong$ _____   _____ $\cong$ _____

_____ $\cong$ _____   _____ $\cong$ _____

_____ $\cong$ _____   _____ $\cong$ _____

Quadrilateral $ABCD \cong$ quadrilateral $EFGH$. In quadrilateral $ABCD$, $AB = 16$, $BC = 5w + 7$, $m\angle C = (2z - 1)°$, and $m\angle D = 50°$. In quadrilateral $EFGH$, $EF = 3y + 1$, $FG = 8$, $m\angle G = 80°$, and $m\angle H = (2x)°$. Find the value of the indicated variable.

3. Find the value of w.

_____

4. Find the value of x.

_____

5. Find the value of y.

_____

6. Find the value of z.

_____

Write the proof.

7. Given: Quadrilateral $MNPQ \cong$ quadrilateral $RSTU$; $\overline{MN} \cong \overline{PQ}$

   Prove: $\overline{MN} \cong \overline{TU}$

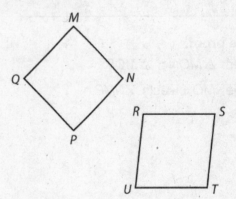

LESSON 18-3

Corresponding Parts of Congruent Figures are Congruent

Practice and Problem Solving: C

1. In rectangle *RSTU*, opposite sides have the same length, and *V* is the midpoint of $\overline{RT}$ and $\overline{SU}$. Find three different pairs of congruent triangles. Write a congruence statement for each pair.

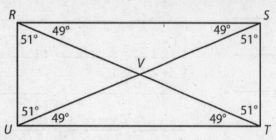

△*ABC* ≅ △*EFG*. Write True or False for each statement. If the statement is false, explain why.

2. The measure of ∠*A* is 45°.

_____

3. The perimeter of △*EFG* is 32.

_____

4. △*ABC* is isosceles.

_____

5. The longest side of △*EFG* is $\overline{FE}$.

_____

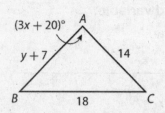

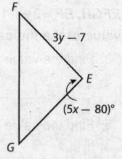

Write the proof.

6. Given: △*MQN* ≅ △*MQP*

   Prove: $\overline{MQ}$ bisects ∠*NMP*

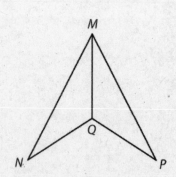

LESSON 19-1

Angles Formed by Intersecting Lines
Practice and Problem Solving: A/B

1. ∠PQR and ∠SQR form a linear pair. Find the sum of their measures. _____

2. Name the ray that ∠PQR and ∠SQR share. _____

Use the figures for Problems 3–8.

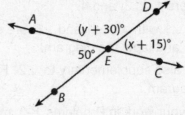

3. supplement of ∠AEB

4. complement of ∠AEB

5. x = _____

6. y = _____

7. m∠DEC = _____

8. m∠AED = _____

9. ∠DEF and ∠FEG are complementary. m∠DEF = (3x − 4)°, and m∠FEG = (5x + 6)°.

   Find the measures of both angles. _____

10. ∠DEF and ∠FEG are supplementary. m∠DEF = (9x + 1)°, and m∠FEG = (8x + 9)°.

    Find the measures of both angles. _____

Use the figure for Problems 11 and 12.

In 2004, several nickels were minted to commemorate the Louisiana Purchase and Lewis and Clark's expedition into the American West. One nickel shows a pipe and a hatchet crossed to symbolize peace between the American government and Native American tribes.

11. Name a pair of vertical angles.

    _____

    _____

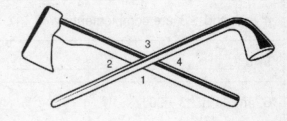

12. Name a linear pair of angles.

    _____

13. ∠ABC and ∠CBD form a linear pair and have equal measures. Tell if

    ∠ABC is acute, right, or obtuse. _____

14. ∠KLM and ∠MLN are complementary. $\overline{LM}$ bisects ∠KLN. Find the

    measures of ∠KLM and ∠MLN. _____

Angles Formed by Intersecting Lines

LESSON 19-1

Practice and Problem Solving: C

Draw your answers in the space provided.

1. Draw two intersecting lines and label the resulting angles with the numbers 1, 2, 3, and 4.

2. Label ∠1 with *x*°. ∠1 and ∠2 are supplementary. Find the measure of ∠2 and label the diagram.

3. ∠3 is also supplementary to ∠2. Find the measure of ∠3 and label the diagram.

4. From your work in Problems 1–3, make a conclusion about the measures of the vertical angles.

5. The diagram shows a light ray passing through a thin pane of glass. The ray hits the glass at ∠1 to the surface. It then moves out the other side at ∠2 to the surface so that ∠1 and ∠2 form vertical angles.

   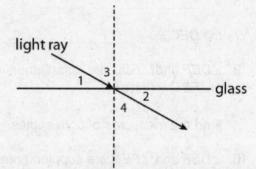

   Write a two-column proof showing that if ∠1 and ∠3 are complementary, and ∠2 and ∠4 are complementary, then m∠3 = m∠4.

Statements	Reasons
1. ∠1 and ∠2 are vertical angles.	1. Given
2. a. _____	2. Vertical Angle Theorem
3. b. _____	3. Definition of Congruent Angles
4. ∠1 and ∠3 are complementary.	4. Given
5. c. _____	5. d. _____
6. m∠1 + m∠3 = 90°	6. Definition of Complementary Angles
7. e. _____	7. f. _____
8. g. _____	8. Substitution Property
9. m∠3 = m∠4	9. h. _____

LESSON
19-2

Transversals and Parallel Lines

Practice and Problem Solving: A/B

Find each angle measure.

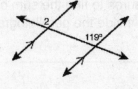

1. m∠1 _____

2. m∠2 _____

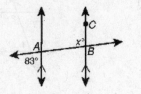

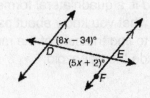

3. m∠ABC _____

4. m∠DEF _____

Complete the two-column proof to show that same-side exterior angles are supplementary.

5. **Given:** p ∥ q

   Prove: m∠1 + m∠3 = 180°

   Proof:

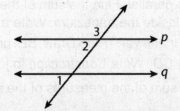

Statements	Reasons
1. p ∥ q	1. Given
2. a. _____	2. Lin. Pair Thm.
3. ∠1 ≅ ∠2	3. b. _____
4. c. _____	4. Def. of ≅ ∠
5. d. _____	5. e. _____

6. Ocean waves move in parallel lines toward the shore. The figure shows Sandy Beaches windsurfing across several waves. For this problem, think of Sandy's wake as a line. m∠1 = (2x + 10)° and m∠2 = (4y – 30)°. Find x and y.

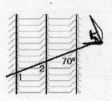

   x = _____

   y = _____

LESSON 19-2

Transversals and Parallel Lines

Practice and Problem Solving: C

1. A *parallelogram* is a quadrilateral formed by two pairs of parallel lines. Use what you know about parallel lines and angle measures to find the sum of the measures of the four angles inside the parallelogram. Explain your answer.

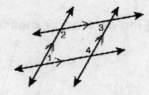

_____

_____

2. A *trapezoid* is a quadrilateral formed by one pair of parallel lines. Use what you know about parallel lines and angle measures to find the sum of the measures of the four angles inside the trapezoid.

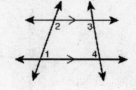

_____

3. A *trapezium* is a quadrilateral formed by four lines, no two of which are parallel. Find the sum of the measures of the four angles inside the trapezium. Write a two-column proof to justify your answer. (*Hint:* Draw $\overline{BE}$ parallel to $\overline{AD}$ and having E on $\overline{CD}$. Write *Construction* to justify this step.)

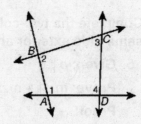

Given: The sum of the measures of the angles in a triangle is 180°.

Prove: m∠1 + m∠2 + m∠3 + m∠4 = _____

_____

_____

_____

_____

_____

_____

_____

_____

Name _____ Date _____ Class_____

LESSON
19-3
Proving Lines Are Parallel
Practice and Problem Solving: A/B

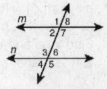

Use the figure for Problems 1–8. Tell whether lines *m* and *n* must be parallel from the given information. If they are, state your reasoning. (*Hint:* The angle measures may change for each problem, and the figure is for reference only.)

1. $\angle 7 \cong \angle 3$

2. $m\angle 3 = (15x + 22)°$, $m\angle 1 = (19x - 10)°$, $x = 8$

_____

3. $\angle 7 \cong \angle 6$

4. $m\angle 2 = (5x + 3)°$, $m\angle 3 = (8x - 5)°$, $x = 14$

_____

5. $m\angle 8 = (6x - 1)°$, $m\angle 4 = (5x + 3)°$, $x = 9$

6. $\angle 5 \cong \angle 7$

_____

7. $\angle 1 \cong \angle 5$

8. $m\angle 6 = (x + 10)°$, $m\angle 2 = (x + 15)°$

_____

9. Look at some of the printed letters in a textbook. The small horizontal and vertical segments attached to the ends of the letters are called *serifs*. Most of the letters in a textbook are in a serif typeface. The letters on this page do not have serifs, so these letters are in a sans-serif typeface. (*Sans* means "without" in French.) The figure shows a capital letter *A* with serifs. Use the given information to write a paragraph proof that the serif, segment $\overline{HI}$, is parallel to segment $\overline{JK}$.

Given: $\angle 1$ and $\angle 3$ are supplementary.

Prove: $\overline{HI} \parallel \overline{JK}$

Name _____ Date _____ Class _____

**LESSON
19-3**

Proving Lines Are Parallel
Practice and Problem Solving: C

1. $p \parallel q$, $m\angle 1 = (6x + y - 4)°$, $m\angle 2 = (x - 9y + 1)°$, $m\angle 3 = (11x + 2)°$
Find x, y, and the measures of $\angle 1$, $\angle 2$, and $\angle 3$.

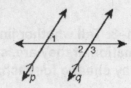

_____

2. A definition of parallel lines is "two coplanar lines that never intersect."
Imagine railroad tracks or the strings on a guitar. Another way to think
about parallel lines is that they extend in exactly the same direction.
Or to say it more mathematically, if a third line intersects one line in a
right angle and intersects a second line in a right angle, then the first
and second lines are parallel. Use this last definition as the final step in
a paragraph proof of the following.

Given: The sum of the angle measures in any
triangle is 180°; $\angle 1 \cong \angle 2$

Prove: $\overrightarrow{AB}$ and $\overrightarrow{CD}$ are parallel lines.

(*Hint*: First draw line $\overrightarrow{AE}$ so it forms a 90° angle with $\overrightarrow{AB}$.
This step can be justified by the Protractor Postulate.
On the figure, label the intersection of $\overrightarrow{AE}$ and $\overrightarrow{CD}$ point F.)

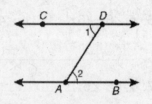

_____
_____
_____
_____
_____
_____
_____

3. $s \parallel t$, $m\angle 1 = (3x - 6)°$, $m\angle 2 = (5x + 2y)°$,
$m\angle 3 = (x + y + 6)°$; Find x, y, and the measures
of $\angle 1$, $\angle 2$, and $\angle 3$.

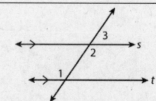

_____
_____

LESSON 19-4

Perpendicular Lines

Practice and Problem Solving: A/B

For Problems 1–2, determine the unknown values.

1. Given: $\overleftrightarrow{AC}$ is the perpendicular bisector of $\overline{GH}$.

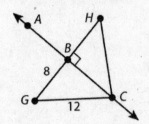

GH = _____

CH = _____

2. Given: $\overleftrightarrow{CD}$ is the perpendicular bisector of $\overline{PR}$.

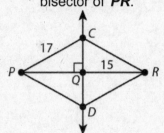

CR = _____

PQ = _____

Complete the two-column proof.

3. **Given:** $m \perp n$

   Prove: $\angle 1$ and $\angle 2$ are a linear pair of congruent angles.

   Proof:

Statements	Reasons
1. a. _____	1. Given
2. b. _____	2. Def. of $\perp$
3. $\angle 1 \cong \angle 2$	3. c. _____
4. $m\angle 1 + m\angle 2 = 180°$	4. Add. Prop. of =
5. d. _____	5. Def. of linear pair

4. The Four Corners National Monument is at the intersection of the borders of Arizona, Colorado, New Mexico, and Utah. It is called the four corners because the intersecting borders are perpendicular. If you were to lie down on the intersection, you could be in four states at the same time—the only place in the United States where this is possible. The figure shows the Colorado–Utah border extending north in a straight line until it intersects the Wyoming border at a right angle. Explain why the Colorado–Wyoming border must be parallel to the Colorado–New Mexico border.

_____

_____

_____

Perpendicular Lines

LESSON 19-4

Practice and Problem Solving: C

1. Draw a segment a little more than half the width of this page. Label this segment with length x, then use a compass and straightedge to construct a segment that has length $\dfrac{5}{4}x$.

2. Among segments $\overline{BA}$, $\overline{BC}$, $\overline{BD}$, and $\overline{BE}$, which is the shortest segment in the figure? Name the second-shortest segment. Explain your answers.

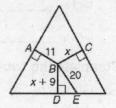

_____

_____

_____

_____

3. Use a straightedge to draw a triangle. Construct the perpendicular bisector of each side of the triangle, and extend the bisectors into the interior of the triangle. Mark the point of intersection of the three bisectors. This is the *circumcenter* of the triangle. Use your compass to compare the distance from the circumcenter to each vertex of the triangle. What is remarkable about the distances?

_____

Now construct a circle completely around the triangle through all three vertices with your compass. You have *circumscribed* a circle around a triangle.

4. An architect designs a triangular jogging track around a circular pond. Each side of the track just touches the pond. The circle is *inscribed* in the triangle. The center of the circle is called the *incenter* of the triangle. The diameter of the circle has length 41.

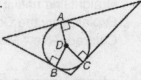

$DA = 8x + 2z - 1\dfrac{1}{2}$, $DB = 6x + y + 1$, $DC = 11y - 2z + 2$.

Find x, y, and z.

Name _____ Date _____ Class_____

LESSON 19-5

Equations of Parallel and Perpendicular Lines

Practice and Problem Solving: A/B

Find the rise and the run between the marked points on each graph. Then find the slope of the line.

1.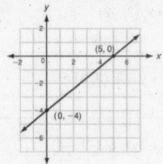

rise = _____ run = _____

slope = _____

2.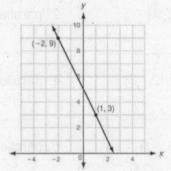

rise = _____ run = _____

slope = _____

3.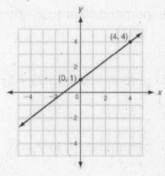

rise = _____ run = _____

slope = _____

Write an equation parallel to the given line through the given point.

4. parallel to $y = 9x + 4$
   through $(2, 7)$

   _____

5. parallel to $y = 4x - 6$
   through $(6, -3)$

   _____

6. parallel to $y = \frac{2}{3}x + 6$
   through $(-3, 6)$

   _____

7. parallel to $y = -\frac{1}{4}x - 12$
   through $(12, 10)$

   _____

Write an equation perpendicular to the given line through the given point.

8. perpendicular to $y = \frac{1}{4}x + 3$
   through $(4, 1)$

   _____

9. perpendicular to $y = -\frac{1}{3}x - 6$
   through $(-2, 8)$

   _____

10. perpendicular to $y = -6x - 9$
    through $(6, 10)$

    _____

11. perpendicular to $y = 5x + 14$
    through $(5, -3)$

    _____

Equations of Parallel and Perpendicular Lines

Practice and Problem Solving: C

Write the equation of the line that is parallel or perpendicular to the graph of the given equation and that passes through the given point.

1. perpendicular to $x - 6y = 2$; (2, 4)

   _____

2. parallel to $y = x$; (7, −2)

   _____

3. perpendicular to $2x + 5y = -3$; (2, −3)

   _____

4. parallel to $5x + y = 2$; (2, 3)

   _____

5. perpendicular to $y = 3x - 2$; (6, −1)

   _____

6. parallel to $9x + 3y = 8$; (−1, −4)

   _____

For Problems 7–8, write the equation of the line that passes through (2, 7) and is perpendicular to the given line.

7. $y = -5$

   _____

8. $x = -5$

   _____

9. A line that passes through the points (2, 1) and (k, 5) is perpendicular to the line $y = 3x - 9$. Find the value of k.

   _____

10. The graphs of the equations $2x + 5y = 3$ and $2x + 5y = 7$ are parallel lines. Find the equation of the line that is parallel to both lines and lies midway between them.

   _____

11. A line on the coordinate plane passes through the points (7, −5) and (3, 11). A line that is perpendicular to the first line passes through the points (−3, −9) and (5, n). Find the value of n.

   _____

12. A line that passes through the points (2, −3) and (b, 7) is parallel to the line $y = -2x + 17$. Find the value of b.

   _____

13. The lines $x = 0$, $y = 2x - 5$, and $y = mx + 9$ form a right triangle. Find two possible values of m.

   _____

LESSON 20-1

Exploring What Makes Triangles Congruent

Practice and Problem Solving: A/B

$\triangle XYZ \cong \triangle NPQ$. **Identify the congruent corresponding parts.**

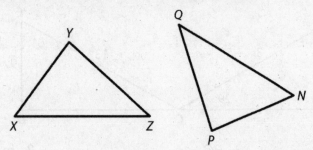

1. $\angle Z \cong$ _____

2. $\overline{YZ} \cong$ _____

3. $\angle P \cong$ _____

4. $\angle X \cong$ _____

5. $\overline{NQ} \cong$ _____

6. $\overline{PN} \cong$ _____

$\triangle LMN \cong \triangle CBA$. **Find each value.**

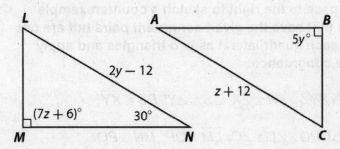

7. $z =$ _____

8. $y =$ _____

9. $m\angle L =$ _____

10. $LN =$ _____

11. $m\angle C =$ _____

12. $AC =$ _____

$\triangle QRS \cong \triangle JKL$.

13. Mark all the congruent corresponding parts of the two triangles.

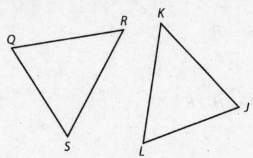

LESSON 20-1

Exploring What Makes Triangles Congruent

Practice and Problem Solving: C

$\triangle ABC \cong \triangle EDC$. $BD = 24$. Find each value.

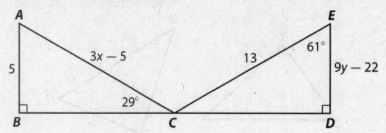

1. $m\angle A =$ _____
2. $BC =$ _____
3. $m\angle DCE =$ _____
4. $ED =$ _____
5. $x =$ _____
6. $y =$ _____

For each question below, two figures are named, and pairs of congruent parts of the figures are given. Write $\cong$ in the blank if the figures are definitely congruent. If there is not enough information, write ? and use the space to the right to sketch a counterexample showing two figures that have the given congruent pairs but are not congruent. Think of each quadrilateral as two triangles and apply principles of triangle congruence.

7. $\triangle RST$ _____ $\triangle XYZ$: $\angle R \cong \angle X$; $\angle S \cong \angle Y$; $\overline{RS} \cong \overline{XY}$

8. $\triangle LMN$ _____ $\triangle OPQ$: $\angle L \cong \angle O$; $\overline{LM} \cong \overline{OP}$; $\overline{MN} \cong \overline{PQ}$

9. $ABCD$ _____ $EFGH$: $m\angle A = m\angle E = 90°$;

   $m\angle B = m\angle F = 90°$; $\overline{AD} \cong \overline{EH}$; $\overline{AB} \cong \overline{EF}$

10. $STUV$ _____ $WXYZ$: $m\angle S = m\angle W = 90°$;

   $m\angle U = m\angle Y = 90°$; $\overline{ST} \cong \overline{WX}$; $\overline{TU} \cong \overline{XY}$

11. $JKLM$ _____ $NPQR$: $\angle J \cong \angle N$; $\angle K \cong \angle P$;

   $\angle L \cong \angle Q$; $\overline{KL} \cong \overline{PQ}$

12. $CDEF$ _____ $GHIJ$: $\angle C \cong \angle G$; $\angle D \cong \angle H$; $\angle E \cong \angle J$;

   $\overline{CD} \cong \overline{GH}$; $\overline{DE} \cong \overline{HI}$; $\overline{EF} \cong \overline{IJ}$

LESSON 20-2
ASA Triangle Congruence
Practice and Problem Solving: A/B

Apply ASA Triangle Congruence to answer Problems 1–3.

1. What additional information do you need in order to conclude that △PQS ≅ △RQS? Explain your reasoning.

   _____

   _____

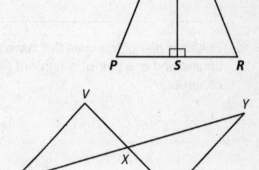

2. Point X is the midpoint of $\overline{VZ}$. Can you conclude that △VWX is congruent to △ZYX? If so, explain your answer. If there is not enough information, explain what additional information is needed.

   _____

   _____

3. Angle D of △DEF is congruent to ∠G of △GHJ. Angle E is congruent to ∠H. Side DE is congruent to side HJ. Can you prove that the two triangles are congruent? Explain your answer.

   _____

   _____

For Problems 4 and 5, use the figure to the right.

4. Complete the proof to prove that △ABC ≅ △CDA.

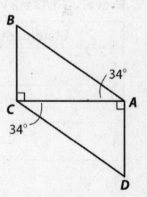

Statements	Reasons
1. ∠ACD ≅ ∠_____	1.
2.	2. Given
3.	3.
4. △ABC ≅ △CDA	4.

5. Describe a sequence of two rigid motions that maps △ABC ≅ △CDA.

   _____

   _____

LESSON 20-2
ASA Triangle Congruence
Practice and Problem Solving: C

Apply ASA Triangle Congruence to answer Problems 1–3.

1. In the figure, *MP* bisects ∠*NMQ* and ∠*NPQ*. Explain
   how you know that *MN* = *MQ*.

   _____

   _____

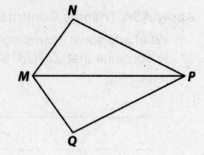

2. Sketch a pair of triangles that have two pairs of congruent
   angles and one pair of congruent sides and are *not*
   congruent.

3. In the figure, *LN* bisects ∠*KLM*. Explain how you know
   that ∠*K* ≅ ∠*M*.

   _____

   _____

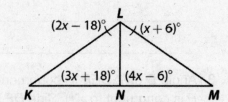

For Problem 4, use the figure to the right.

4. **Given:** ∠*PQU* ≅ ∠*TSU*; ∠*QUR* and ∠*SUV* are right angles; *QU* = *SU*
   Prove: ∠*RUQ* ≅ ∠*VUS*

Statements	Reasons
1.	1.
2.	2.
3.	3.
4.	4.
5.	5.
6.	6.

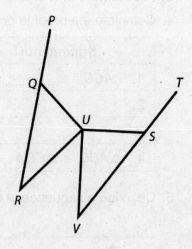

Name _____ Date _____ Class_____

LESSON 20-3
SAS Triangle Congruence
Practice and Problem Solving: A/B

Use principles of triangle congruence to answer Problems 1 and 2.

1. If you know the leg lengths of two right triangles, can you tell whether they are congruent? Explain your answer.

_____

_____

_____

2. If two triangles have three pairs of congruent parts, will they always be congruent? Explain your answer.

_____

_____

_____

For Problems 3 and 4, use the figure at the right.

3. Explain how you know that △ABD ≅ △CBD.

_____

_____

_____

A ——————— B
29°
61°
11 cm   11 cm
61°
D 29°   C

4. Describe a sequence of two rigid motions that maps △ABD onto △CBD.

_____

_____

Use the figure at the right for the two-column proof.

5. The Hatfields and the McCoys are feuding over some land. Neither family will be satisfied unless the two triangular fields are exactly the same size. Point C is the midpoint of each of the intersecting segments. Write a two-column proof that will settle the dispute.

Given: C is the midpoint of $\overline{AD}$ and $\overline{BE}$.

Prove: △ABC ≅ △DEC

Statements	Reasons
1. C is the _____ of _____ and _____.	1. _____
2. AC = CD, _____ = _____	2. Definition of _____
3. $\overline{AC} \cong \overline{CD}$, _____ ≅ _____	3. Definition of _____
4. ∠ACB ≅ ∠_____	4. _____
5. _____ ≅ _____	5. _____

LESSON
20-3

SAS Triangle Congruence
Practice and Problem Solving: C

Use principles of triangle congruence for Problems 1–3.

1. In the figure, *O* is the center of the circle and ∠*DOE* ≅ ∠*FOE*.
   Explain how you know that $\overline{DE} \cong \overline{EF}$.

   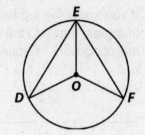

   _____

   _____

2. In the figure, *M* bisects $\overline{AC}$ and $\overline{BD}$. Also, ∠*BDA* ≅ ∠*CAD*.
   Explain how you know that ∠*B* ≅ ∠*C*.

   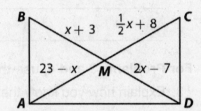

   _____

   _____

3. Draw two perpendicular segments, $\overline{QS}$ and $\overline{RT}$, such that
   $\overline{QS}$ bisects $\overline{RT}$ at point *U*. Draw figure *QRST*. Identify
   the congruent triangles formed by the figure and its
   diagonals, and tell how you know they are congruent.

   _____

Use the figure to the right to do the two-column proof.

4. **Given:** $\overline{GH} \cong \overline{KL}$; $\overline{GH} \parallel \overline{KL}$; $\overline{FL} \cong \overline{JH}$

   Prove: ∠*FGH* ≅ ∠*JKL*

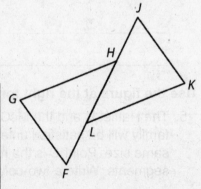

Statements	Reasons
1.	1.
2.	2.
3.	3.
4.	4.
5.	5.
6.	6.
7.	7.

LESSON 20-4

SSS Triangle Congruence

Practice and Problem Solving: A/B

Use principles of congruence to answer Problems 1–3.

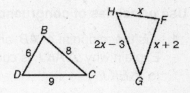

1. Show that △BCD is congruent to △FGH if x = 6.

_____

_____

2. In the figure, $\overline{AB} \cong \overline{AD}$. Explain how you know that $\angle B \cong \angle D$.

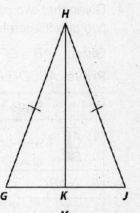

_____

_____

_____

3. In the figure, *H* is equidistant from the endpoints of line segment $\overline{GJ}$. Leon said that means that $\overleftrightarrow{HK}$ is the perpendicular bisector of $\overline{GJ}$. Was he right? Explain your reasoning.

_____

_____

_____

Use the figure at the right for the two-column proof.

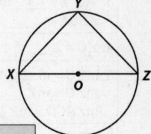

4. Point *O* is the center of the circle. The chords $\overline{XY}$ and $\overline{ZY}$ are congruent. Fill in the missing statements and reasons to prove that $\angle X$ is congruent to $\angle Z$.

Given: Circle *O*, $\overline{XY} \cong \overline{ZY}$

Prove: $\angle X \cong \angle Z$

Statements	Reasons
1. $\overline{XY} \cong \overline{ZY}$	1.
2.	2.
3.	3. Reflexive property of congruence
4.	4.
5.	5.

LESSON 20-4

SSS Triangle Congruence

Practice and Problem Solving: C

Use principles of congruence for Problems 1–3.

1. *J* is the midpoint of *AB*, and $\overline{AK} \cong \overline{BK}$. Explain why △*AKJ* is congruent to △*BKJ*.

_____

_____

_____

_____

2. Can a square be determined given only the length of a diagonal? Explain your answer.

_____

_____

_____

_____

3. The two triangles in the figure are congruent. Find the total area of the figure. _____ sq ft

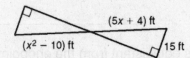

Complete the two-column proof.

4. Given that two pairs of corresponding sides and three pairs of corresponding angles of two quadrilaterals are congruent, prove that the quadrilaterals are congruent.

Given: $\overline{AB} \cong \overline{EF}$; $\angle B \cong \angle F$; $\overline{BC} \cong \overline{FG}$; $\angle C \cong \angle G$; $\angle D \cong \angle H$

Prove: *ABCD* ≅ *EFGH*

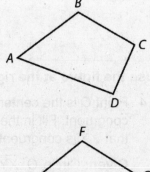

Statements	Reasons
1. $\overline{AB} \cong$ ____; $\angle B \cong$ ____; $\overline{BC} \cong$ ____	1.
2. △*ABC* ≅ △ ____	2.
3. $\overline{AC} \cong \angle$ ____ and $\angle BCA \cong \angle$ ____	3.
4. $\angle C \cong \angle$ ____	4.
5. $m\angle C = m\angle BCA + m\angle$ ____ $m\angle G = m\angle$ ____ $+ m\angle$ ____ $m\angle ACD = m\angle$ ____	5. Angle addition
6. $\angle D \cong \angle$ ____	6.
7. △*ACD* ≅ △ ____	7.
8. $\overline{CD} \cong \angle$ ____ and $\overline{AD} \cong \angle$ ____	8.
9.	9. All corresponding parts are congruent.

LESSON 21-1

Justifying Constructions

Practice and Problem Solving: A/B

The figure shows the construction line and arcs for drawing the angle bisector of ∠ABC.

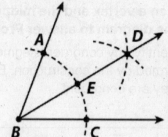

1. Name a point on the construction that is the same distance from D as A is.

   _____

2. Name a line segment that is congruent to $\overline{AB}$.

   _____

3. Suppose you drew segments $\overline{AD}$ and $\overline{DC}$. Which angle congruence theorem could you use to prove that $\triangle BAD \cong \triangle BCD$? Explain your reasoning.

   _____

   _____

   _____

T is in the interior of ∠PQR. A student constructs $\overrightarrow{QT}$ so that it bisects ∠PQR. Find each of the following.

4. m∠PQR if m∠RQT = 11° _____

5. m∠PQR if m∠RQT = $(5x - 7)°$ and m∠PQT = $(4x + 6)°$ _____

6. m∠TQR if m∠RQT = $(10x - 13)°$ and m∠PQT = $(6x + 1)°$ _____

The figure shows △FGH, an isosceles triangle, constructed so that $GH = FH$ and $\overline{GL}$ and $\overline{FL}$ are angle bisectors. Find each of the following quantities.

7. m∠FGL = _____

8. m∠GFL = _____

9. m∠GLF = _____

10. Joseph constructed two parallel lines and labeled the angles formed so that ∠3 and ∠7 were corresponding. He labeled m∠3 as $(5x + 3)°$ and m∠7 as 68°. What is the value of x?

   _____

Justifying Constructions

LESSON 21-1

Practice and Problem Solving: C

The diagram below shows how to construct one of the
medians of the triangle. A median is a line segment
between a vertex and the midpoint of the opposite side.
Use the diagram to answer Problem 1.

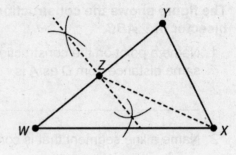

1. Identify any congruent segments and angles
   formed by the construction. Explain how you know
   they are congruent.

   _____

   _____

   _____

2. The figure at the right shows the result if the construction
   is completed and the midpoints are connected. Describe
   three pairs of congruent angles in the figure. Then identify
   the theorem that proves that they are congruent.

   _____

   _____

   _____

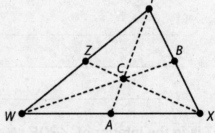

3. In an isosceles triangle, at least two of the angles are congruent. To
   construct isosceles triangle *DEH*, begin by drawing $\overrightarrow{DE}$ and $\overrightarrow{DF}$. If
   you copy ∠*FDE* and let the angle open in the same direction, the ray
   would be parallel to $\overrightarrow{DF}$. Instead, copy ∠*FDE* and draw $\overrightarrow{EG}$ so that
   the ray intersects $\overrightarrow{DF}$. Label the intersection point *H*. Measure $\overline{DH}$
   and $\overline{EH}$. What is remarkable about the lengths of these segments?

   _____

   _____

   _____

   _____

LESSON
21-2

AAS Triangle Congruence
Practice and Problem Solving: A/B

1. Students in Mrs. Marquez's class are watching a film on the uses of geometry in architecture. The film projector casts the image on a flat screen as shown in the figure. The dotted line is the bisector of $\overline{AC}$. Can you use the AAS Theorem to prove that $\triangle ABD \cong \triangle CBD$? Explain why or why not.

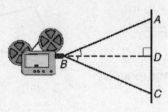

_____

_____

Write whether the AAS Congruence Theorem, the ASA Congruence Theorem, or neither can be used to prove the pair of triangles congruent.

2.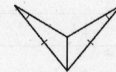

3.

_____

_____

4.

5.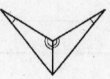

_____

_____

Write a paragraph proof.

6. **Given:** $\angle PQU \cong \angle TSU$
    $\angle QUR$ and $\angle SUR$ are right angles.
   Prove: $\triangle RUQ \cong \triangle RUS$

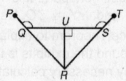

_____

_____

_____

AAS Triangle Congruence

Practice and Problem Solving: C

Explain the mistake in each proof in Problems 1–2. Then describe a correct way to prove that the triangles are congruent. Identify any additional information that is needed.

1. Given: $\overline{FD} \parallel \overline{BC}$, $\overline{AB} \parallel \overline{DE}$, and $\overline{AC} \cong \overline{FE}$

   Since $\overline{FD} \parallel \overline{BC}$, $\angle DFE \cong \angle ACB$ by the Alt. Int. $\angle$ Thm. Since $\overline{AB} \parallel \overline{DE}$, $\angle ABC \cong \angle EDF$ by the Alt. Int. $\angle$ Thm. Also, $\overline{AC} \cong \overline{FE}$ is given. Therefore, $\triangle ABC \cong \triangle EDF$ by AAS Congruence Theorem.

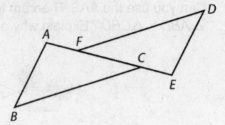

   Mistake: _____

   _____

2. Given: $\overline{AC} \cong \overline{CD}$; $\angle ACB$ and $\angle ECD$ are vertical angles.

   Since $\angle ACB$ and $\angle ECD$ are vertical angles, $\angle ACB \cong \angle ECD$ by the Vert. Angle Thm. $\overline{AC} \cong \overline{CD}$ is given. Since $\overline{AB} \parallel \overline{DE}$, $\angle ABC \cong \angle EDC$. Therefore, $\triangle ABC \cong \triangle DEC$ by AAS Congruence Theorem.

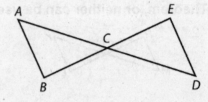

   Mistake: _____

   _____

Solve.

3. The grid shows the outlines of two exhibit areas at an amusement park. It is known that $\angle X \cong \angle P$ and $\angle Y \cong \angle Q$. Use the AAS Congruence Theorem to explain why the distance around the exhibits is the same. Make any necessary calculations.

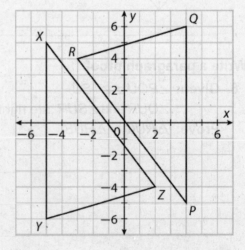

Name _____ Date _____ Class_____

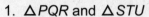

LESSON
21-3

HL Triangle Congruence

Practice and Problem Solving: A/B

For Problems 1–3, use the HL Congruence Theorem to determine if the given triangles are congruent. For Problems 2 and 3, make sure the triangles are right triangles. Explain your answers.

1. △*PQR* and △*STU*

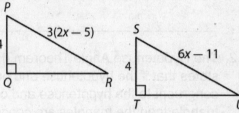

_____

_____

_____

2. *A*(–2, 2); *B*(4, –4); *C*(–2, –4); *D*(1, –1)
   △*ACD* and △*BCD*

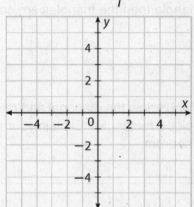

_____

_____

_____

3. *A*(0, 2); *B*(–4, 0); *C*(0, –3); *D*(–2, 1)
   △*ACD* and △*BCD*

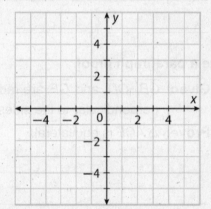

_____

_____

_____

4. Complete the proof.

   Given: isosceles triangle △*PQS* with $\overline{PQ} \cong \overline{PS}$

   and $\overline{PR} \perp \overline{QS}$

   Prove: △*PQR* ≅ △*PSR*

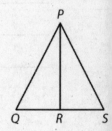

Statements	Reasons
1.	1. Given
2. ∠*PRQ* and ∠*PRS* are right angles.	2.
3.	3. Definition of right triangle
4.	4.
5.	5.

Name _____ Date _____ Class_____

HL Triangle Congruence
Practice and Problem Solving: C

1. In what cases is knowing three parts (side lengths or angle measures)
   of a triangle not sufficient information to determine a specific triangle?

   _____

   _____

2. The Hypotenuse Angle Theorem (HA), similar to the HL Theorem,
   states that if the hypotenuse and one angle of a right triangle are
   congruent to the hypotenuse and corresponding angle of another right
   triangle then the triangles are congruent. Prove the HA Theorem.

   _____

   _____

3. If you know the diagonal and one side of a rectangle, can you draw a
   unique rectangle? Explain your answer and relate it to the HL
   Theorem.

   _____

   _____

   _____

Write a paragraph proof.

4. **Given:** $\overline{GB}$, $\overline{GD}$, and $\overline{GF}$ are radii of the circle centered at G and are
   perpendicular to the sides of $\triangle ACE$.

   Prove: $\triangle ACE$ is equilateral.

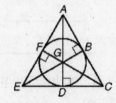

   _____

   _____

   _____

   _____

LESSON 22-1

Interior and Exterior Angles
Practice and Problem Solving: A/B

Find the measure of each angle.

1.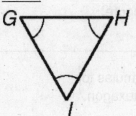

   m∠B = _____°

2.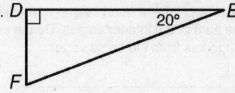

   m∠F = _____°

3.

   m∠G = _____°

4.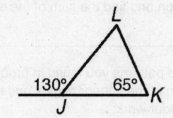

   m∠L = _____°

5.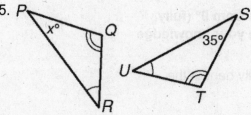

   m∠P = _____°

6.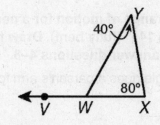

   m∠VWY = _____°

Use your knowledge of angle relationships to answer questions 7–12.

7. The sum of the angle measures of a quadrilateral is _____°.

8. The acute angles of a _____ triangle are complementary.

9. The measure of an _____ angle of a triangle is equal to the sum
   of the measures of its remote interior angles.

10. The angle measures of a triangle are *a*, 3*a*, and 5*a*. Tell the measure
    of each angle. _____°, _____°, _____°

11. You know that one of the exterior angles of an isosceles triangle is

    140°. The angle measures of the triangle could be _____°-_____°-

    _____° or _____°-_____°-_____°.

Name _____ Date _____ Class_____

LESSON
22-1

Interior and Exterior Angles
Practice and Problem Solving: C

Use your knowledge of interior and exterior angles to answer questions 1–3.

1. Draw and label a quadrilateral with one diagonal and show how to find the sum of the interior angles. Do the same for a pentagon with two diagonals from the same vertex.

   _____

2. Draw one exterior angle at each vertex of a quadrilateral and of a pentagon and find the sum of the exterior angles for each figure.

   _____

3. Use the patterns you found in problems 1 and 2 to write formulas for the sum of the interior angles and the exterior angles of a hexagon. Show your work.

   _____

The normal range of motion for a person's elbow is from 0° (fully extended) to 145° (fully bent). Draw figures and use your knowledge of angles to answer questions 4–8.

4. What angle does a person's arm form when it is fully bent at the

   elbow? _____°

5. Consider the triangle formed by Jared's elbow, the tips of his fingers when his arm is fully extended, and the tips of his fingers when his arm

   is fully bent. Name the angles of this triangle. _____°, _____°, _____°

6. After Ella broke her elbow, her maximum extension was 8°, and her maximum flexion was 136°. How many degrees of range of motion did

   she lose? _____°

7. With normal range of motion, a person can touch his or her shoulder with the fingers by bending the elbow and wrist. (Try it.) Given the measures below, use a protractor and ruler to draw and label a figure to illustrate this situation.

   shoulder to fingertips: 30 in.   elbow to wrist: 10 in.
   elbow to fingertips: 18 in.   flexion of wrist: 90°

8. Can Ella touch her shoulder with her fingers? Using the measurements in question 7 and Ella's flexion after breaking her arm, draw a figure and explain your answer.

   _____

LESSON 22-2

Isosceles and Equilateral Triangles

Practice and Problem Solving: A/B

For Problems 1–6, find each value.

1.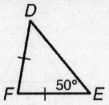

   m∠D = _____°

2.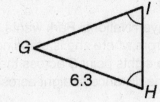

   GI = _____

3.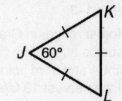

   m∠L = _____°

4.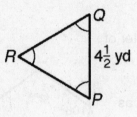

   RQ = _____

5.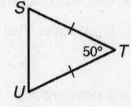

   m∠U = _____°

6.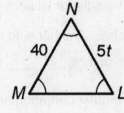

   t = _____

Use principles of isosceles and equilateral triangles to answer Problems 7–9.

7. Point *M* lies on side *JL* of triangle *JKL*. $\overline{KM}$ bisects $\overline{JL}$ and forms

   equilateral triangle *KLM*. What is the measure of ∠J? _____°

   Make a sketch and explain your answer. _____

   _____

   _____

8. Circle *B* and circle *C* are congruent. Point *A* is an
   intersection of the two circles. Write a paragraph
   proof to show that △*ABC* is equilateral.

   _____

   _____

   _____

   _____

   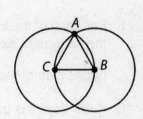

9. The Washington Monument is an *obelisk,* a tall, thin, four-sided
   monument that tapers to a pyramidal top. Each face of the pyramidal
   top of the Washington Monument is an isosceles triangle. The height
   of each triangle is 55.5 feet, and the base of each triangle measures
   34.4 feet. Find the length, to the nearest tenth of a foot, of one of the

   two congruent legs of the triangle. _____ ft

Name _____ Date _____ Class_____

LESSON 22-2 **Isosceles and Equilateral Triangles**
Practice and Problem Solving: C

Use principles of isosceles and equilateral triangles to solve Problems 1–3.

1. A forest ranger in Grand Canyon National Park wants to find the distance across the canyon from where she is standing. From point A and from point C, she sights point B across the canyon. To the nearest 10 feet, find the distance straight across the canyon,

   from D to B. _____ ft

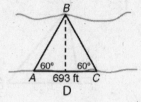

2. A triangle for billiards is equiangular. One side measures $(2x + 1)$ inches. Another side measures $(4x - 9\frac{1}{4})$ inches. Find the perimeter of the triangle. _____ in.

3. A regular pentagon has five congruent sides and five 108° angles, as shown in the figure. Find the angle measures: $x =$ _____; $y =$ _____;

   $z =$ _____

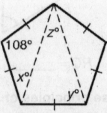

David and Kellie have a piece of wood that is 30 inches square. They want to cut it to make a small tabletop in the shape of a regular octagon.

4. David says that a regular octagon is composed of eight isosceles triangles, so he suggests that they draw the four lines of symmetry and mark off the triangles. Draw a line to show where to make one of the cuts. Give the angle measures for the isosceles triangles.

   _____°, _____°, _____°

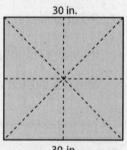

5. For each of the isosceles triangles, the ratio of the length of one of the congruent sides to the length of the base is 1.3. Tell the length of one side of the octagon to the nearest 0.1 inch. _____ in.

6. Kellie says it is possible to make a bigger regular octagon from the wood. Mark the figure to show how to make the biggest octagon possible. Explain your reasoning and tell the length of one side of the octagon. _____ in.

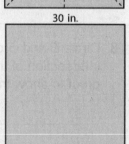

Quadratic Formula

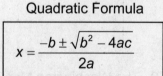

$$x = \frac{-b \pm \sqrt{b^2 - 4ac}}{2a}$$

Original content Copyright © by Houghton Mifflin Harcourt. Additions and changes to the original content are the responsibility of the instructor.
158

LESSON
22-3

Triangle Inequalities
Practice and Problem Solving: A/B

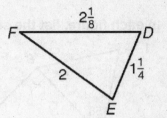

For Problems 1–3, name the angles or sides.

1. Write the angles of △*DEF* in order from smallest to largest.

   ∠_____   ∠_____   ∠_____

2. Write the sides of △*GHI* in order from shortest to longest.

   _____   _____   _____

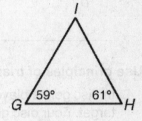

3. The sides of triangle *XYZ* are given in order below from longest to shortest. Name the angles from largest to smallest.

   $\overline{XZ}$ $\overline{ZY}$ $\overline{YX}$

   ∠_____   ∠_____   ∠_____

Use your knowledge of triangle inequalities to solve Problems 4–7.

4. Can three segments with lengths 8, 15, and 6 make a triangle? Explain

   your answer. _____

   _____

5. For an isosceles triangle with congruent sides of length *s*, what is the range of lengths for the base, *b*? What is the range of angle measures, *A*, for the angle opposite the base? Write the inequalities and explain

   your answers. _____

   _____

6. Aaron, Brandon, and Clara sit in class so that they are at the vertices of a triangle. It is 15 feet from Aaron to Brandon, and it is 8 feet from Brandon to Clara. Give the range of possible distances, *d*, from Aaron

   to Clara. _____

7. Renaldo plans to leave from Atlanta and fly into London (4281 miles). On the return, he will fly back from London to New York City (3470 miles) to visit his aunt. Then Renaldo heads back to Atlanta. Atlanta, New York City, and London do not lie on the same line. Find the range

   of the total distance Renaldo could travel on his trip. _____

   _____

LESSON
22-3

Triangle Inequalities

Practice and Problem Solving: C

In each figure, list the segments in order from longest to shortest.

1.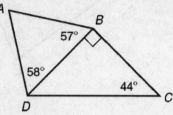

2.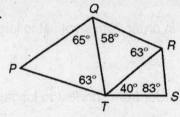

3.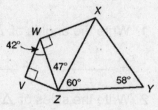

_____   _____   _____

Use principles of triangle inequalities to solve Problems 4 and 5.

4. In disc golf, a player tries to throw a disc into a metal basket target. Four disc golf targets on a course are shown at right.

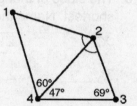

   Which two targets are closest together? _____

   Which two targets are farthest apart? _____

5. Name the shortest segment in the figure and explain your reasoning. Do not use a ruler. (*Note*: The figure may not be drawn to scale.)

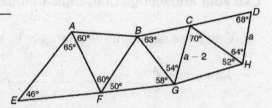

_____

_____

_____

Describe how you could prove the theorem.

6. Unequal Sides Theorem
   Given: △ABC with BC > AB
   Prove: m∠ BAC > m∠C
   Plan for proof: Locate point D on $\overline{BC}$ such that BD = BA. Draw $\overline{AD}$.
   Explain why m∠BAC > m∠3, m∠3 > m∠C, and so m∠BAC > m∠C.

_____

_____

_____

_____

_____

LESSON 23-1

Perpendicular Bisectors of Triangles

Practice and Problem Solving: A/B

Use the figure for Problems 1–4.

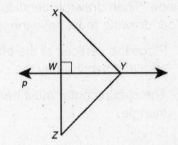

1. Given that line *p* is the perpendicular bisector of $\overline{XZ}$

   and *XY* = 15.5, find *ZY*. _____

2. Given that *XZ* = 38, *YX* = 27, and *YZ* = 27,

   find *ZW*. _____

3. Given that line *p* is the perpendicular bisector of $\overline{XZ}$,

   XY = 4*n*, and *YZ* = 14, find *n*. _____

4. Given that *XY* = *ZY*, *WX* = 6*x* − 1, and *XZ* = 10*x* + 16, find *ZW*. _____

Use the figure for Problems 5–6. $\overline{SV}$, $\overline{TV}$, and $\overline{UV}$ are
perpendicular bisectors of the sides of △*PQR*. Find each length.

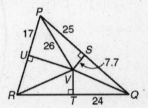

5. *RV* _____   6. *TR* _____

Find the circumcenter of the triangle with the given vertices.

7. *A*(0, 0), *B*(0, 5), *C*(5, 0)   8. *D*(0, 7), *E*(−3, 1), *F*(3, 1)

   (_____, _____)   (_____, _____)

Use the graph of △*ABC* to complete Problems 9–15.

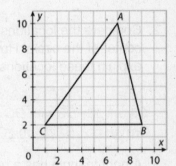

9. Draw a perpendicular bisector to $\overline{CB}$ on the graph.

10. Use the midpoint formula to determine the

    midpoint of $\overline{AC}$. _____

11. What is the slope of $\overline{AC}$? _____

12. What is slope of a line perpendicular to

    $\overline{AC}$? _____

13. Use the point-slope form to find the equation

    of the perpendicular bisector of $\overline{AC}$. _____

14. Draw the perpendicular bisector of $\overline{AC}$.

15. What is the point where the lines intersect called? _____

Name _____ Date _____ Class _____

Perpendicular Bisectors of Triangles
Practice and Problem Solving: C

1. Use construction tools to draw two different triangles within the circle
   below. Then draw perpendicular bisectors to each side of the triangles.
   Your drawing must have these properties:

   • Place the vertices of the triangles on the circle so that the triangles
     are circumscribed by the circle.

   • The circumcenter must be outside one triangle and inside the other
     triangle.

2. Compare the locations of the circumcenters of the triangles to the
   center of the circle. How does the length of each radius of a circle
   explain these locations?

   _____

   _____

3. A right triangle has a hypotenuse with length 17. What is the radius of

   the circle that can be circumscribed about this triangle? _____

4. $\overline{VS}$, $\overline{VT}$, and $\overline{VU}$ are perpendicular bisectors of the sides
   of △PQR. Find the circumference of the circle that can be
   circumscribed about this triangle.

   _____

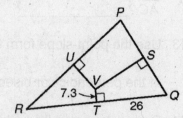

LESSON
23-2

Angle Bisectors of Triangles
Practice and Problem Solving: A/B

Use the figure for Problems 1–4.

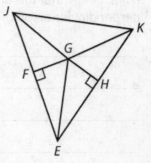

1. Given that $FG = HG$ and m$\angle FEH = 55°$, find

   m$\angle GEH$. _____

2. Given that $\overline{EG}$ bisects $\angle FEH$ and $GF = \sqrt{2}$, find GH.

   _____

3. Given that $\angle FEG \cong \angle GEH$, $FG = 10z - 30$, and

   $HG = 7z + 6$, find FG. _____

4. Given that $GF = GH$, m$\angle GEF = \dfrac{8}{3}a°$, and m$\angle GEH = 24°$, find a. _____

Use the figure for Problems 5–9. $\overline{GJ}$ and $\overline{IJ}$ are angle bisectors of $\triangle GHI$. Find each measure.

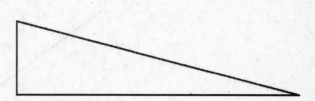

5. m$\angle JGK$ _____

6. m$\angle JIK$ _____

7. m$\angle KJI$ _____

8. the distance from J to $\overline{GH}$ _____

9. the distance from J to $\overline{IH}$ _____

Solve.

10. Raleigh designs the interiors of cars. The triangular surface shown in the figure is molded into the driver's side door as an armrest. Raleigh thinks he can fit a cup holder into the triangle, but he'll have to put the largest possible circle into the triangle. Explain how Raleigh can do this. Sketch his design on the figure.

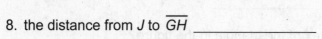

_____

_____

_____

_____

**LESSON
23-2**

Angle Bisectors of Triangles

Practice and Problem Solving: C

1. Draw a diagram and write a paragraph proof showing that the incenter
   and the circumcenter are the same point for an equilateral triangle.
   (*Hint:* Show that the angle bisector is the same line as the
   perpendicular bisector, or vice versa.)

   _____

   _____

   _____

   _____

   _____

   _____

   _____

2. Meteor Crater in northern Arizona was created by the
   impact of a relatively small meteor—about 80 feet in
   diameter. The figure shows the distances if the
   landowners at Meteor Crater built an equilateral
   triangle-shaped roadway around the crater. Find the
   diameter of the crater produced by the meteor.

   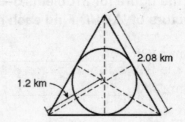

   _____

3. Construct angle bisectors from each vertex of the triangle in the figure,
   and mark the point where the bisectors intersect. Use this point as the
   center of a circle with a radius equal to the perpendicular distance from
   the center to one of the sides.

   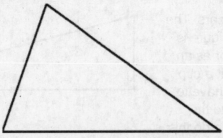

4. $\overline{KH}$ and $\overline{KJ}$ are angle bisectors of $\triangle HIJ$. Find the area
   of the circle that can be inscribed in this triangle.

   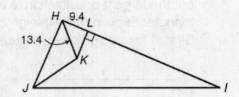

   _____

LESSON
23-3

Medians and Altitudes of Triangles

Practice and Problem Solving: A/B

Use the figure for Problems 1–4. $GB = 12\frac{2}{3}$ and $CD = 10$.

Find each length.

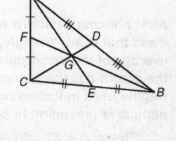

1. *FG* _____

2. *BF* _____

3. *GD* _____

4. *CG* _____

5. A triangular compass needle will turn most easily if it is attached to the compass face through its centroid. Find the coordinates of the centroid.

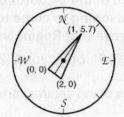

(_____, _____)

Find the orthocenter of the triangle with the given vertices.

6. *X*(–5, 4), *Y*(2, –3), *Z*(1, 4)

(_____, _____)

7. (0, –1), *B*(2, –3), *C*(4, –1)

(_____, _____)

Use the figure for Problems 8 and 9. $\overline{HL}, \overline{IM},$ and $\overline{JK}$ are medians of △*HIJ*. Round answers to the nearest tenth, if necessary.

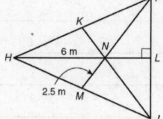

8. Find the area of the triangle. _____

9. What is *HJ*? _____

10. What is the perimeter? _____

11. Two medians of a triangle were cut apart at the centroid to make the four segments shown below. Use what you know about the Centroid Theorem to reconstruct the original triangle from the four segments shown. Measure the side lengths of your triangle to check that you constructed medians. (*Note:* There are many possible answers.)

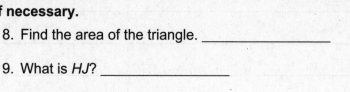

LESSON 23-3

Medians and Altitudes of Triangles
Practice and Problem Solving: C

1. In a right triangle, what kind of line connects the
   orthocenter and the circumcenter? _____

**After noticing a pattern with several triangles, Regina declares to her
class that in any triangle, the *x*-coordinate of the centroid is the
average of the *x*-coordinates of the vertices, and the *y*-coordinate of
the centroid is the average of the *y*-coordinates of the vertices.
Regina used inductive reasoning to come to her conclusion. Use
deductive reasoning to prove that Regina's conclusion is correct.**

2. **Given:** $\triangle ABC$ with $A(0, 0)$, $B(2b, 2c)$, $C(2a, 0)$

   Prove: The coordinates of the centroid are $\left(\dfrac{2a + 2b}{3}, \dfrac{2c}{3}\right)$.

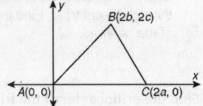

_____

_____

_____

_____

_____

_____

_____

_____

_____

_____

_____

_____

_____

_____

_____

_____

_____

LESSON
23-4
Midsegments of Triangles
Practice and Problem Solving: A/B

Use the figure for Problems 1–6. Find each measure.

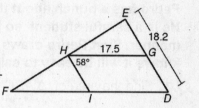

1. *HI* _____

2. *DF* _____

3. *GE* _____

4. m∠*HIF* _____

5. m∠*HGD* _____

6. m∠*D* _____

The Bermuda Triangle is a region in the Atlantic Ocean off the southeast coast of the United States. The triangle is bounded by Miami, Florida; San Juan, Puerto Rico; and Bermuda. In the figure, the dotted lines are midsegments.

	Dist. (mi)
Miami to San Juan	1038
Miami to Bermuda	1042
Bermuda to San Juan	965

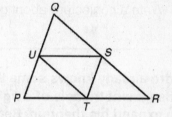

7. Use the distances in the chart to find the perimeter of the Bermuda Triangle.

_____

8. Find the perimeter of the midsegment triangle within the Bermuda Triangle.

_____

9. How does the perimeter of the midsegment triangle compare to the perimeter of the Bermuda Triangle?

_____

Write a two-column proof that the perimeter of a midsegment triangle is half the perimeter of the triangle.

10. **Given:** $\overline{US}$, $\overline{ST}$, and $\overline{TU}$ are midsegments of △*PQR*.

  Prove: The perimeter of $\triangle STU = \frac{1}{2}(PQ + QR + RP)$.

_____

_____

_____

_____

_____

_____

_____

_____

_____

LESSON
23-4

Midsegments of Triangles

Practice and Problem Solving: C

Pedro has a hunch about the area of midsegment triangles. He is a careful student, so he investigates in a methodical manner. First Pedro draws a right triangle because he knows it will be easy to calculate the area.

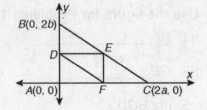

1. Find the area of △ABC. _____

2. Find the coordinates of the midpoints *D*, *E*, and *F*. _____

3. Pedro knows it will be easy to find the area of △EFD if ∠DEF is a right angle. Write a proof that ∠DEF ≅ ∠A.

4. Find the area of △EFD. _____

5. Compare the areas of △ABC and △EFD.

_____

6. Pedro has already shown that △EFD ≅ △ADF. Calculate the area of △ADF. _____

7. Write a conjecture about congruent triangles and area.

_____

Pedro already knows some things about the area of the midsegment triangle of a right triangle. But he thinks he can expand his theorem. Before he can get to that, however, he has to show another property of triangles and area.

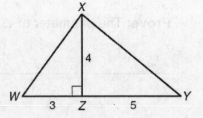

8. Find the area of △WXY, △WXZ, and △YXZ.

_____

9. Compare the total of the areas of △WXZ and △YXZ to the area of △WXY.

_____

_____

10. Write a conjecture about the areas of triangles within a larger triangle.

_____

_____

LESSON 24-1

Properties of Parallelograms
Practice and Problem Solving: A/B

PQRS is a parallelogram. Find each measure.

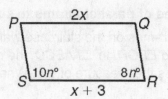

1. *RS* _____

2. m∠*S* _____

3. m∠*R* _____

The figure shows a swing blown to one side by a breeze. As long as the seat of the swing is parallel to the top bar, the swing makes a parallelogram. In □ *ABCD*, *DC* = 2 ft, *BE* = $4\frac{1}{2}$ ft, and m∠*BAD* = 75°.

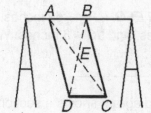

Find each measure.

4. *AB* _____

5. *ED* _____

6. *BD* _____

7. m∠*ABC* _____

8. m∠*BCD* _____

9. m∠*ADC* _____

Three vertices of □ *GHIJ* are *G*(0, 0), *H*(2, 3), and *J*(6, 1). Use the grid to the right to complete Problems 10–16.

10. Plot vertices *G*, *H*, and *J* on the coordinate plane.

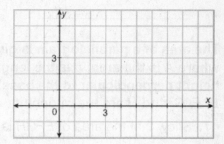

11. Find the rise (difference in the *y*-coordinates) from

    G to *H*. _____

12. Find the run (difference in the *x*-coordinates) from

    G to *H*. _____

13. Using your answers from Problems 11 and 12, add the rise to the *y*-coordinate of vertex *J* and add the run to the *x*-coordinate of vertex *J*.

    The coordinates of vertex *I* are (_____, _____).

14. Plot vertex *I*. Connect the points to draw □ *GHIJ*.

15. Check your answer by finding the slopes of $\overline{IH}$ and $\overline{JG}$.

    slope of $\overline{IH}$ = _____ slope of $\overline{JG}$ = _____

16. What do the slopes tell you about $\overline{IH}$ and $\overline{JG}$? _____

_____

LESSON
24-1

Properties of Parallelograms

Practice and Problem Solving: C

Use properties of parallelograms to solve Problems 1–3.

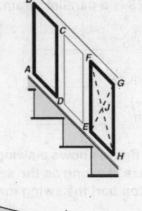

1. The wall frames on the staircase wall form parallelograms *ABCD* and *EFGH*. In □ *ABCD*, the measure of ∠A is three times the measure of ∠B. What are the measures

   of ∠C and ∠D? _____ ; _____

2. In □ *EFGH*, *FH* = 5x inches, *EG* = (2x + 4) inches, and *JG* = 8 inches. What is the length of *JH*?

   _____

3. The diagram shows a section of the support structure of a roller coaster. In □ *JKLM*, *JK* = (3z − 0.9) feet and

   LM = (z + 2.7) feet. Find *JK*. _____

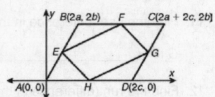

Find the range of possible diagonal lengths in a parallelogram with the given side lengths.

4. 3 and 12   5. x and 2x   6. x and x

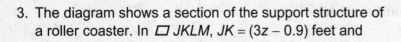

The area of a parallelogram is given by the formula *A = bh*, where *A* is the area, *b* is the length of a base, and *h* is the height perpendicular to the base. *ABCD* is a parallelogram. *E, F, G,* and *H* are the midpoints of the sides.

7. Show that the area of *EFGH* is half the area of *ABCD*.

8. Show that *EFGH* is a parallelogram.

LESSON 24-2

Conditions for Parallelograms

Practice and Problem Solving: A/B

Determine whether each figure is a parallelogram for the given values of the variables. Explain your answers.

1. $x = 9$ and $y = 11$

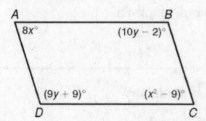

2. $a = 4.3$ and $b = 13$

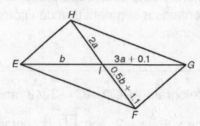

_____

_____

_____

_____

_____

_____

A quadrilateral has vertices $E(1, 1)$, $F(4, 5)$, $G(6, 6)$, and $H(3, 2)$. Complete Problems 3–6 to determine whether $EFGH$ is a parallelogram.

3. Plot the vertices and draw $EFGH$.

4. Use the Pythagorean Theorem to find the lengths of

   sides $\overline{EF}$ and $\overline{HG}$. $EF =$ _____ $HG =$ _____

5. Use the Slope Formula to find the slopes of sides $\overline{EF}$ and

   $\overline{GH}$. slope of $\overline{EF} =$ _____ slope of $\overline{HG} =$ _____

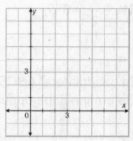

6. The answers to Problems 4 and 5 reveal important information about figure $EFGH$. State the theorem that uses the information found to prove that $EFGH$ is a parallelogram.

   _____

   _____

Use the given method to determine whether the quadrilateral with the given vertices is a parallelogram.

7. Find the slopes of all four sides: $J(-4, -1)$, $K(-7, -4)$, $L(2, -10)$, $M(5, -7)$.

   _____

   _____

8. Find the lengths of all four sides: $P(2, 2)$, $Q(1, -3)$, $R(-4, 2)$, $S(-3, 7)$.

   _____

   _____

Name _____ Date _____ Class_____

LESSON 24-2

Conditions for Parallelograms

Practice and Problem Solving: C

Use properties of parallelograms to solve Problems 1–4.

1. The graphs of $y = 2x$, $y = 2x - 5$, and $y = -x$ contain three sides of a quadrilateral in the coordinate plane. Give an equation of a line whose graph contains a segment that can complete the quadrilateral to form a parallelogram.

   _____

2. In parallelogram $ABCD$, $AC = 3\sqrt{13}$ and $BD = 5\sqrt{5}$. $\overline{AC}$ is contained in the line $y = \dfrac{3}{2}x - 2$, and $\overline{BD}$ is contained in the line $y = \dfrac{11}{2}x - 6$.

   If A and B are both in Quadrant I, find the vertices of $ABCD$.

   (*Hint:* All coordinates are integers.) _____

3. Find the slopes and lengths of one pair of opposite sides of quadrilateral $TUVW$. Is the figure a parallelogram with vertices $T\left(\dfrac{3}{2}, -2\right)$, $U\left(\dfrac{3}{2}, 4\right)$, $V\left(-\dfrac{1}{2}, 0\right)$,

   $W\left(-\dfrac{1}{2}, -6\right)$?

   _____

4. In quadrilateral $ABCD$, $\angle A \cong \angle B$ and $\angle C \cong \angle D$. Is it possible to determine if the opposite sides of the figure are parallel? Explain.

   _____

Write a two-column proof.

5. If the diagonals of a parallelogram are perpendicular and congruent, the figure is a square. (Diagonals intersect at point E.)

   Given: $ABCD$ is a parallelogram. $\overline{AC}$ and $\overline{BD}$ are perpendicular and congruent.

   Prove: $ABCD$ is a square.

Statements	Reasons
1.	1.
2.	2.
3.	3.
4.	4.
5.	5.
6.	6.
7.	7.

Name _____ Date _____ Class_____

LESSON 24-3
Properties of Rectangles, Rhombuses, and Squares
Practice and Problem Solving: A/B

Tell whether each figure is a parallelogram, rectangle, rhombus, or square based on the information given. Use the most specific name possible.

1. 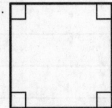   2. 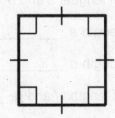   3. 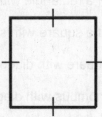   4.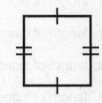

_____ _____ _____ _____

A modern artist's sculpture has rectangular faces. The face shown here is 9 feet long and 4 feet wide. Find each measure in simplest radical form. (*Hint:* Use the Pythagorean Theorem.)

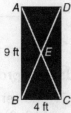

5. DC = _____   6. AD = _____

7. DB = _____   8. AE = _____

VWXY is a rhombus. Find each measure.

9. XY = _____

10. m∠YVW = _____

11. m∠VYX = _____

12. m∠XYZ = _____

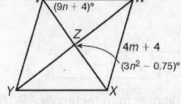

Write a paragraph proof.

13. **Given:** ABCD is a rectangle.
    Prove: ∠EDC ≅ ∠ECD

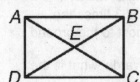

_____

_____

_____

_____

_____

_____

Original content Copyright © by Houghton Mifflin Harcourt. Additions and changes to the original content are the responsibility of the instructor.

173

Properties of Rectangles, Rhombuses, and Squares

LESSON 24-3

Practice and Problem Solving: C

For Problems 1–6, find the measures of the given figures.
For Problems 1–5, give your answers in simplest radical form.

1. length of diagonals of a rectangle with sides of lengths *a* and *b* _____

2. length of diagonals of a square with sides of length *s* _____

3. length of sides of a square with diagonals of length *d* _____

4. length of sides of a rhombus with diagonals of lengths *f* and *g* _____

5. length of a rectangle with width *w* and a diagonal of length 2*w* _____

6. measures of angles in the triangles formed by one diagonal of
   the rectangle in Problem 5.
   Explain how you found your answer. _____

   _____

   _____

Use the properties of special parallelograms to solve Problems 7 and 8.

7. The vertices of square *JKLM* are *J*(–2, 4), *K*(–3, –1), *L*(2, –2), and
   M(3, 3). Find each of the following to show that the diagonals of square
   JKLM are congruent perpendicular bisectors of each other.

   JL = _____   *KM* = _____

   slope of $\overline{JL}$ = _____   slope of $\overline{KM}$ = _____

   midpoint of $\overline{JL}$ = (_____, _____)   midpoint of $\overline{KM}$ = (_____, _____)

8. The soccer goalposts form rectangle *ABCD*. The
   distance between goalposts, *BC*, is 3 times the
   distance from the top of the goalpost to the ground.

   If the perimeter of *ABCD* is $21\frac{1}{3}$ yards, what is the

   length of diagonal $\overline{BD}$, to the nearest tenth of a foot? _____

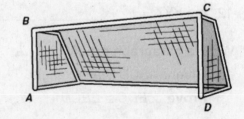

Write a paragraph proof for the statement.

9. If one pair of opposite angles of a quadrilateral are congruent and the
   diagonal bisects both angles, then the other diagonal bisects the other
   two angles.

   _____

   _____

   _____

LESSON 24-4

Conditions for Rectangles, Rhombuses, and Squares

Practice and Problem Solving: A/B

Fill in the blanks to complete each theorem.

1. If one pair of consecutive sides of a parallelogram are congruent, then

   the parallelogram is a _____.

2. If the diagonals of a parallelogram are _____, then
   the parallelogram is a rhombus.

3. If the _____ of a parallelogram are congruent, then
   the parallelogram is a rectangle.

4. If one diagonal of a parallelogram bisects a pair of opposite angles,

   then the parallelogram is a _____.

5. If one angle of a parallelogram is a right angle, then the parallelogram

   is a _____.

Use the figure for Problems 6–7. Determine whether each conclusion is valid. If not, tell what additional information is needed to make it valid.

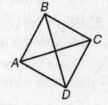

6. **Given:** $\overline{AC}$ and $\overline{BD}$ bisect each other. $\overline{AC} \cong \overline{BD}$

   Conclusion: *ABCD* is a square.

   _____

7. **Given:** $\overline{AC} \perp \overline{BD}, \overline{AB} \cong \overline{BC}$

   Conclusion: *ABCD* is a rhombus.

   _____

Complete Problems 8–11 to show that the conclusion is valid.

Given: $\overline{JK} \cong \overline{ML}, \overline{JM} \cong \overline{KL}$, and $\overline{JK} \cong \overline{KL}$. $\angle M$ is a right angle.

Conclusion: *JKLM* is a square.

8. Because $\overline{JK} \cong \overline{ML}$ and $\overline{JM} \cong \overline{KL}$, *JKLM* is a _____.

9. Because *JKLM* is a parallelogram and $\angle M$ is a right angle, *JKLM* is a

   _____.

10. Because *JKLM* is a parallelogram and $\overline{JK} \cong \overline{KL}$, *JKLM* is a _____.

11. Because *JKLM* is a _____ and a _____,
    JKLM is a square.

LESSON 24-4

Conditions for Rectangles, Rhombuses, and Squares
Practice and Problem Solving: C

1. Of a parallelogram, rectangle, rhombus, or square, name the two that can have a diagonal congruent to a side. Explain your reasoning.

_____

_____

_____

2. Of the two quadrilaterals you named in Problem 1, with a diagonal congruent to a side, tell which one's diagonal length can be determined unambiguously given a side length (using only what you have learned in this geometry course so far). _____

3. If the congruent side and diagonal of the special quadrilateral from Problem 2 have length *x*, find the length of the other diagonal. _____

4. Give the measures of the interior angles of the special quadrilateral from Problem 2. _____

5. Given the coordinates of three vertices of a parallelogram, tell how many parallelograms can be formed. _____

6. Given the coordinates of three vertices of a rectangle, tell how many rectangles can be formed. _____

7. Given the coordinates of three vertices of a rhombus, tell how many rhombuses can be formed. _____

8. Given the coordinates of three vertices of a square, tell how many squares can be formed. _____

9. Given the coordinates of two vertices of a parallelogram, rectangle, or rhombus, tell how many of each can be formed. _____

10. Given the coordinates of two vertices of a square, tell how many squares can be formed. _____

11. Tell how many points are sufficient to determine a parallelogram. _____

12. Tell how many points are sufficient to determine a rectangle, a rhombus, or a square. _____

13. Find all the possible coordinates of the fourth vertex of a parallelogram with vertices (2, 3), (3, 0), and (4, 4). _____

14. Plot the three vertices given in Problem 13.
Connect the vertices to make a triangle.
Then plot the coordinates of all the possible fourth vertices. Connect these vertices.
Name the relationship of the original triangle to the new figure you created.

_____

LESSON 24-5

Properties and Conditions for Kites and Trapezoids

Practice and Problem Solving: A/B

In kite *ABCD*, m∠*BAC* = 35° and m∠*BCD* = 44°.
For Problems 1–3, find each measure.

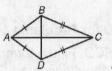

1. m∠*ABD*

2. m∠*DCA*

3. m∠*ABC*

_____   _____   _____

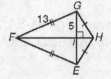

4. Find the area of △*EFG*. _____

5. Find m∠*Z*.

6. *KM* = 7.5 and *NM* = 2.6. Find *LN*.

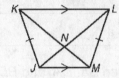

7. Find the value of *n* so that *PQRS* is isosceles.

_____

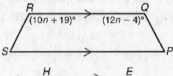

8. Find the values of *x* so that *EFGH* is isosceles.

_____

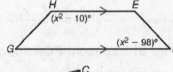

9. *BD* = 7*a* − 0.5 and *AC* = 5*a* + 2.3. Find the value of *a* so that *ABCD* is isosceles.

_____

10. *QS* = 8*z*², and *RT* = 6*z*² + 38. Find the values of *z* so that *QRST* is isosceles.

_____

Use the figure for Problems 11 and 12. The figure shows a *ziggurat*. A ziggurat is a stepped, flat-topped pyramid that was used as a temple by ancient peoples of Mesopotamia. The dashed lines show that a ziggurat has sides roughly in the shape of a trapezoid.

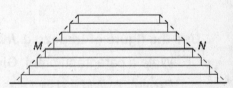

11. Each "step" in the ziggurat has equal height. Give the vocabulary term for $\overline{MN}$.

_____

12. The bottom of the ziggurat is 27.3 meters long, and the top of the ziggurat is 11.6 meters long. Find *MN*.

_____

LESSON 24-5

Properties and Conditions for Kites and Trapezoids

Practice and Problem Solving: C

Use the figure of kite *ABCD* for Problems 1–3.

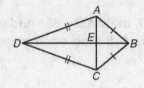

1. The figure shows kite *ABCD*. Find a formula for the area of a kite in terms of the diagonals *AC* and *BD*.

   _____

2. Suppose you are given *BA*, *AC*, and *ED*. Tell whether it is possible to find the area of *ABCD*. Explain your answer.

   _____

   _____

   _____

3. Suppose you are given *BA*, *DA*, and *BD*. Tell whether it is possible to find the area of *ABCD* (with what you have learned so far in this geometry class). Explain your answer.

   _____

   _____

Use the figure of trapezoid *PQRS* for Problem 4.

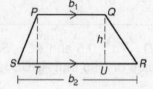

4. Write a paragraph proof.

   Given: $\overline{PQ} \parallel \overline{SR}$, $\overline{QU} \perp \overline{SR}$, $\overline{PT} \perp \overline{SR}$

   Prove: *PQUT* is a rectangle.

Use the figure of trapezoid *JKLM* for Problem 5.

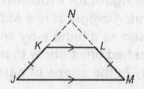

5. Write a paragraph proof. **Given:** Isosceles trapezoid *JKLM*

   Prove: $\triangle JNM$ is isosceles.

Name _____ Date _____ Class_____

LESSON
25-1

Slope and Parallel Lines

Practice and Problem Solving: A/B

Line *A* contains the points (2, 6) and (4, 10). Line *B* contains the points (–2, 3) and (3, 13).

1. Are the lines parallel? Explain your reasoning.

_____

_____

Figure *JKLM* has as its vertices the points *J*(4, 4), *K*(2, 1), *L*(–3, 2), and *M*(–1, 5).

Find each slope.

2. $\overline{JK}$ 3. $\overline{KL}$ 4. $\overline{LM}$ 5. $\overline{MJ}$

_____   _____   _____   _____

6. Is *JKLM* a parallelogram? Explain your reasoning.

_____

_____

For Problems 7–10, use the graph at the right.

7. Find the slope of line ℓ.

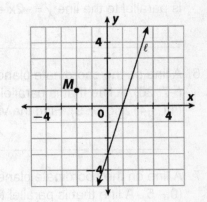

_____

8. Explain how you found the slope.

_____

_____

9. Line *m* is parallel to line ℓ and passes through point *M*.
   Find the slope of line *m*.

_____

10. Find the equation of line *m*. Explain how you found the equation.

_____

_____

_____

LESSON
25-1

Slope and Parallel Lines

Practice and Problem Solving: C

Write the equation of the line that is parallel to the graph of the given equation and that passes through the given point.

1. $y = -6x + 4$; $(-2, 3)$

2. $y = x$; $(7, -2)$

_____   _____

3. Quadrilateral *ABCD* has vertices $A(-1, 5)$, $B(4, 0)$, $C(1, -5)$, and $D(-5, 1)$. Calculate the slopes of the sides, and then use your results to explain whether *ABCD* is or is not a parallelogram.

_____

_____

_____

4. Find the equation of the line parallel to $2x + 5y = 3$ and $2x + 5y = 7$ that lies midway between them.

_____

5. A line that passes through the points $(2, -3)$ and $(b, 7)$ is parallel to the line $y = -2x + 17$. Find the value of *b*.

_____

6. A line on the coordinate plane passes through the points $(-7, 8)$ and $(-7, 20)$. A line that is parallel to the first line passes through the points $(11, -4)$ and $(x, 9)$. Find the value of *x*.

_____

7. A line on the coordinate plane passes through the points $(-3, -7)$ and $(0, -5)$. A line that is parallel to the first line passes through the points $(6, 4)$ and $(-9, y)$. Find the value of *y*.

_____

8. Line *L* has the equation $ax + by = c$. Line *M* is parallel to Line *L*. What is the slope of Line *M*?

_____

LESSON 25-2
Slope and Perpendicular Lines
Practice and Problem Solving: A/B

Line A contains the points (–1, 5) and (1, –3). Line B contains the points (2, 3) and (–2, 2).

1. Are the lines perpendicular? Explain your reasoning.

_____

_____

Figure WXYZ has as its vertices the points W(2, 7), X(5, 6), Y(5, –4), and Z(–1, –2).

Find each slope.

2. $\overline{WX}$ 3. $\overline{XY}$ 4. $\overline{YZ}$ 5. $\overline{ZW}$

_____   _____   _____   _____

6. Is Figure WXYZ a rectangle? Explain your reasoning.

_____

_____

For Problems 7–10, use the graph at the right.

7. Find the slope of line ℓ.

_____

8. Explain how you found the slope.

_____

_____

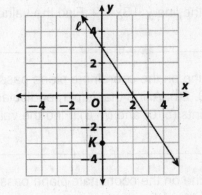

9. Line t is perpendicular to line ℓ and passes through point K.
   Find the slope of line t.

_____

10. Find the equation of line t. Explain how you found the equation.

_____

_____

_____

LESSON 25-2

Slope and Perpendicular Lines

Practice and Problem Solving: C

Write the equation of the line that is perpendicular to the graph of the given equation and passes through the given point.

1. $x - 6y = 2$; (2, 4)

2. $y = -3x + 7$; (-3, 1)

_____

_____

For Problems 3–4, write the equation of the line that passes through the point (2, 7) and is perpendicular to the given line.

3. $y = -5$

4. $x = -5$

_____

_____

5. The sidewalks at a park can be modeled by the equations:
$3(y + 1) = 2x$, $2y - 8 = -3x$, $2x + 3 = 3y$, and $-2(y - 12) = 3x$.
Determine the slopes of the equations, and then use them to
classify the quadrilateral bounded by the sidewalks.

_____

_____

6. A line that passes through the points (2, 1) and (k, 5) is perpendicular
to the line $y = 3x - 9$. Find the value of k.

_____

7. A line on the coordinate plane passes through the points (−3, 8) and
(−9, 20). A line that is perpendicular to the first line passes through the
points (5, 0) and (h, 6). Find the value of h.

_____

8. A line on the coordinate plane passes through the points (7, −5) and
(3, 11). A line that is perpendicular to the first line passes through the
points (−3, −9) and (5, n). Find the value of n.

_____

9. The lines $x = 0$, $y = 2x - 5$, and $y = mx + 9$ form a right triangle. Find
two possible values of m.

_____

LESSON
25-3
Coordinate Proof Using Distance with Segments and Triangles
Practice and Problem Solving: A/B

Position an isosceles triangle with sides of 8 units, 5 units, and
5 units in the coordinate plane. Label the coordinates of each vertex.
(*Hint:* Use the Pythagorean Theorem.)

1. Center the long side on the *x*-axis
   at the origin.

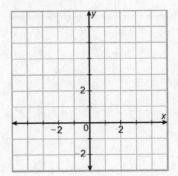

2. Center the long side on the *y*-axis
   at the origin.

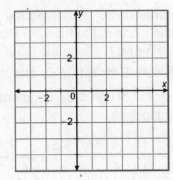

Complete Problems 3–5 to finish the proof.

Given: Triangle *ABC* is an isosceles triangle
with vertices *A*(0, 0), *B*(8, 0), *C*(4, 10). Points
D, E, F are the midpoints of triangle *ABC*.

Prove: Triangle *DEF* is an isosceles triangle.

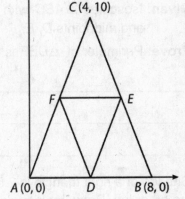

3. Use the midpoint formula to find the coordinates:

   D _____ *E* _____ *F* _____

4. Use the distance formula to show equal side lengths.

   DE = _____ *DF* = _____

5. Suppose, instead, that you want to use △*ABC* to prove
   the Midsegment Theorem, given that $\overline{FE}$ is a midsegment
   and $\overline{AB} \parallel \overline{FE}$. What other steps would you need in the

   coordinate proof? _____

   _____

Coordinate Proof Using Distance with Segments and Triangles

Practice and Problem Solving: C

1. Position an isosceles triangle on the coordinate
   plane at the right so that you can use it for a
   coordinate proof. Place its base on the *x*-axis
   and draw it so that it is symmetric about the *y*-axis.
   Label the vertices $A(2a, 0)$, $B(0, 2b)$, and $C(-2a, 0)$.

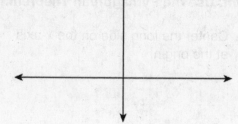

2. Using the vertices given, determine the
   midpoint of each side of the triangle. Plot the
   midpoints on the graph. Place the label *D* for
   side $\overline{AB}$, the label *E* for side $\overline{BC}$, and the
   label *F* for side $\overline{CA}$. Then draw segments to
   connect the midpoints.

   Midpoints: D _____ E _____ F _____

3. Use the graph you have constructed to write a coordinate proof.

   Given: Isosceles $\triangle ABC$ with $AB = BC$
   and midpoints *D, E, F*

   Prove: Perimeter of $\triangle DEF$ is one-half the perimeter of $\triangle ABC$.

   _____

   _____

   _____

4. One leg of a right triangle is 2.5 times the length of
   the other leg. Draw the triangle in the first quadrant
   of the coordinate plane with the legs along the axes
   and a vertex at the origin. Use only integer values
   for your coordinates and write each value as a
   multiple of *a*.

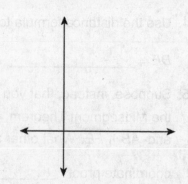

**LESSON
25-4**

Coordinate Proof Using Distance with Quadrilaterals
Practice and Problem Solving: A/B

**Position a trapezoid with parallel sides of 4 units and 6 units in the
coordinate plane. Label the coordinates of each vertex.**

1. Center the long parallel side at the
   origin.

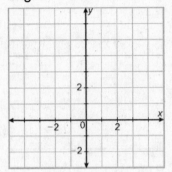

2. Center the long parallel side on the
   y-axis at the origin.

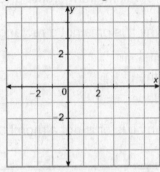

3. Describe the possible steps in a coordinate proof that would show that
   the figure you drew in Problem 1 is a trapezoid.

   _____

   _____

   _____

Write a coordinate proof.

4. **Given:** Rectangle *ABCD* has vertices *A*(0, 4), *B*(6, 4),
   C(6, 0), and *D*(0, 0). *E* is the midpoint of $\overline{DC}$.
   F is the midpoint of $\overline{DA}$.

   Prove: The area of rectangle *DEGF* is one-fourth the
   area of rectangle *ABCD*.

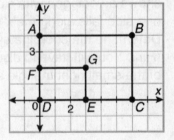

   _____

   _____

   _____

   _____

   _____

   _____

LESSON
25-4

Coordinate Proof Using Distance with Quadrilaterals

Practice and Problem Solving: C

1. A parallelogram has vertices $J(0, -4)$, $K(5, -1)$, $L(4, 4)$, and $M(-1, 1)$.
   Use a coordinate proof to decide whether it is a rectangle, a rhombus,
   or a square. It may be neither, or it may be more than one of these.

   a. Draw the parallelogram on the grid.

   b. Explain why it is or is not a rectangle.

   _____

   _____

   c. Explain why it is or is not a rhombus.

   _____

   _____

   d. Explain why it is or is not a square.

   _____

   _____

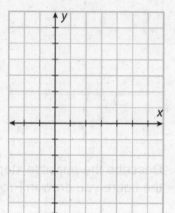

2. A stop sign is a regular octagon. A regular octagon has eight
   congruent sides and eight congruent 135° angles. The figure
   shows an octagon with side length ℓ in a coordinate plane so that
   one side falls along the x-axis and one side falls along the y-axis.
   Determine the coordinates of each vertex in terms of ℓ.
   (*Hint:* You will have to discover a relationship between the sides
   of the small right triangle at the origin.)

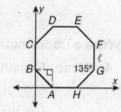

   _____

   _____

3. A "slow down" sign is a regular hexagon. A regular hexagon has
   six congruent sides and six congruent 120° angles. The ℓ figure
   shows a hexagon with side length ℓ in a coordinate plane so that
   one side falls along the x-axis and one vertex falls along the y-axis.
   Determine the coordinates of each vertex in terms of ℓ.

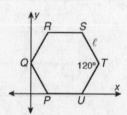

   _____

   _____

LESSON 25-5

Perimeter and Area on the Coordinate Plane

Practice and Problem Solving: A/B

Draw and classify each polygon with the given vertices. Find the perimeter and area of the polygon to the nearest tenth.

1. $A(-2, 3)$, $B(3, 1)$, $C(-2, -1)$, $D(-3, 1)$

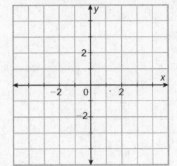

_____

2. $P(-3, -4)$, $Q(3, -3)$, $R(3, -2)$, $S(-3, 2)$

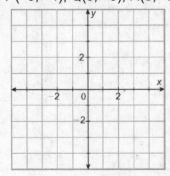

_____

3. $E(-4, 1)$, $F(-2, 3)$, $G(-2, -4)$

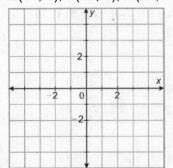

_____

4. $T(1, -2)$, $U(4, 1)$, $V(2, 3)$, $W(-1, 0)$

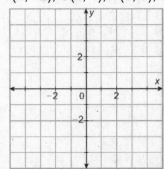

_____

Find the area and perimeter of each composite figure to the nearest tenth.

5.

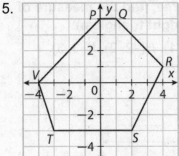

_____

6.

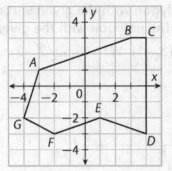

_____

LESSON
25-5
Perimeter and Area on the Coordinate Plane
Practice and Problem Solving: C

Draw each polygon with the given vertices. Find the perimeter and area of the polygon to the nearest tenth.

1. $A(0, 0)$, $B(2, 2)$, $C(-2, 0)$, $D(1, -2)$

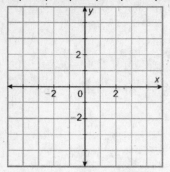

2. $J(2, 4)$, $K(3, -4)$, $L(1, -2)$, $M(-1, -4)$

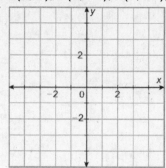

_____

3. $P(-3, 3)$, $Q(1, 2)$, $R(3, -3)$, $S(1, -3)$, $T(-2, -2)$

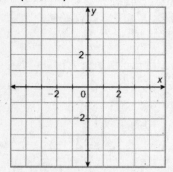

4. $D(2, -1)$, $E(0, 0)$, $F(1, -2)$, $G(0, -4)$, $H(2, -3)$, $I(3, -4)$, $J(3, -2)$, $K(4, 1)$

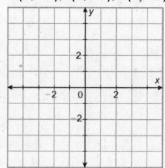

_____

Draw each polygon with the given vertices. To the nearest degree, find the measure of each angle in the polygon with the given vertices. (*Hint:* Form right triangles.)

5. $W(0, 0)$, $X(3, -1)$, $Y(1, -2)$, $Z(-2, -2)$

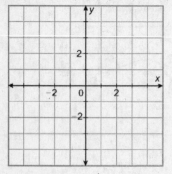

6. $F(3, 4)$, $G(1, 1)$, $H(-2, 2)$, $I(-3, 3)$

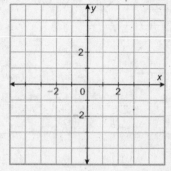

_____

_____